Register This New Book

Benefits of Registering*

- ✓ FREE **replacements** of lost or damaged books
- ✓ FREE **audiobook** – *Pilgrim's Progress*, audiobook edition
- ✓ FREE information about new titles and other **freebies**

www.anekopress.com/new-book-registration

*See our website for requirements and limitations.

THE
Prayer-Meeting
AND ITS
Improvement

"Let all things be done unto edifying." 1 Cor. 14:26

THE
Prayer-Meeting
AND ITS
Improvement

— ❃ —

HOW TO LEAD
CHURCH PRAYER MEETINGS

LEWIS O. THOMPSON
Pastor of Second Presbyterian Church, Peoria, Illinois

With an introduction by
A. E. Kittredge, D. D.

We love hearing from our readers. Please contact us at www.anekopress.com/questions-comments with any questions, comments, or suggestions.

The Prayer-Meeting and Its Improvement
Lewis O. Thompson
Original publication copyright 1878
Please contact us via www.AnekoPress.com for reprint and translation requests regarding this specific edition.
Cover Designer: Jonathan Lewis

Aneko Press
www.anekopress.com
Aneko Press, Life Sentence Publishing, and our logos are trademarks of
Life Sentence Publishing, Inc.
203 E. Birch Street
P.O. Box 652
Abbotsford, WI 54405
RELIGION / Christian Ministry / Pastoral Resources
Paperback ISBN: 978-1-62245-557-7
eBook ISBN: 978-1-62245-558-4
10   9   8   7   6   5   4   3   2   1
Available where books are sold

Contents

Preface to the First Edition ix

Preface to the New Edition xi

Introduction xiii

Ch. 1: The Prayer Meeting as a Subject of Study 1

Ch. 2: The People's Meeting 5

Ch. 3: Preparation 9

Ch. 4: The Daily Cultivation of Piety 15

Ch. 5: The Topics 21

Ch. 6: The Topics Illustrated 27

Ch. 7: One Method for the Selection of Topics 39

Ch. 8: The Bible and the Topics 43

Ch. 9: Bible Readings for the Prayer-Meeting 49

Ch. 10: Illustrations of Bible Readings 53

Ch. 11: A Plan for Each Meeting 65

Ch. 12: Variety in Successive Meetings 73

Ch. 13: The Importance of the Prayer Meeting 77

Ch. 14: How to Make Prayer-Meetings Interesting 81

Ch. 15: Uniform Topics 89

Ch. 16: Steps Towards Uniformity 95

Ch. 17: Helps for Speaking in Public 101

Ch. 18: Aids to Secret, Social, and Public Prayer 109

Ch. 19: The Service of Song 121

Ch. 20: How to Secure Attendance 127

Ch. 21: How Prayer-Meetings are kept at a White Heat 135

Ch. 22: Treatment of the Monthly Concert 139

Ch. 23: Laying out Work 143

Ch. 24: The Social Element in the Prayer-Meeting 149

Ch. 25: Hints New and Old 155

Ch. 26: Daily Prayer-Meeting Topics 161

Bibliography 179

Other Similar Titles 181

Preface to the First Edition

This book is designed as a go-between, between pastor and people, to call their combined attention to some hints and principles that would enlarge the efficiency of the prayer-meeting and to assure those to whom public speaking is a burden, that their experience is common to the majority of mankind and should give them no uneasiness, rather spurring them on until they acquire the habit of impromptu speech.

If the prayer-meeting is to rise into one of the great departments of successful Christian work, there must be as much thought, prayer, and effort given to it as to either of the Sabbath services or the Sabbath-school. What is needed in many cases is such a method for its conduct and such a hearty co-operation of all in that method as shall make the prayer-meeting, both in interest and attendance, an undoubted success.

May the Lord bless for good whatever of truth these chapters contain and make them instrumental in stirring up the zeal of the churches to untiring labor and faithful prayer in the advancement of His cause.

Go little book – if God shall be pleased to commission you – from church to church as an evangelist in the cause of the Prayer-Meeting and its improvement.

Lewis O. Thompson.

Peoria, IL, May 11th, 1878.

Preface to the New Edition

The proof-sheets for the first edition were scarcely out of my hands before Mr. Holmes made arrangements with me for re-issuing the present edition. That a new edition should be called for so soon is a matter of thankfulness for nothing but a slow sale was anticipated for a book on this distinctive theme. Its issue was an experiment and, hence, the book was not electrotyped as it now will be.

As the compositor's work will have to be done over again from the beginning, the opportunity is afforded for revising the entire book and of expanding some of its previous pages into new chapters. Three new chapters and a number of suggestions and footnotes have been added so that, it is hoped, the book in its present permanent form will be found all the more worthy of public favor.

I would here also acknowledge my indebtedness to the press, whose kind remarks have called attention to the book and secured for it a speedier sale than could otherwise have been obtained. Nor should I fail to express my admiration at the conduct of Dr. G. F. Deems, editor of *The Sunday Magazine* and pastor of "The Church of the Strangers," New York City, who, with remarkable generosity, has given up the writing of a book on the same subject with a different title, *The Modern Prayer-Meeting*, so as not to interfere with the circulation of the present volume and because this volume happened to see print a few weeks before his own could have been ready for the press. While this book is highly honored by the withdrawal of competition, it is to be regretted that the public shall be so greatly the losers by this unwonted generosity.

And now I would again commit *The Prayer-Meeting and Its Improvement* to the care of Him who can use even the poorest instrument to the furtherance of His kingdom and the promotion of His glory.

Lewis O. Thompson.

Peoria, IL, June 15th, 1878.

Introduction

It is impossible to over-estimate the value of the prayer-meeting, as it stands related to the life and usefulness of the Church of Christ. In fact, no other service can be compared with this in importance – perhaps not even the Sabbath preaching, nor the instruction in the Sunday-school – for without a live prayer-meeting the church will be spiritually cold, the Sabbath services will be formal, and the children will be fed with husks instead of provisions from the Master's table.

The weekly prayer-meeting is the pulse of the church – one of the most encouraging signs of the times, in the religious world, is the increased interest manifested by pastors and churches in this topic, and the new life and power which now are found in many of these hallowed circles of united prayer and praise. Some of us can remember the prayer-meetings of our childhood, when the number present ranged from ten to twenty or thirty, and most of these were the female members – when the leader occupied most of the hour in cold, doctrinal remarks, and then remarked: "Brethren, the meeting is open," after which came the solemn pauses, only broken by this and that good deacon taking pity on the meeting, and making a few forced and uninteresting remarks. Oh! How cold those meetings were! Cold enough to freeze up any longings to be a Christian, in the breast of a sinner who might have chanced to happen in. How we children used to dread being compelled to attend, preferring even to go to bed earlier than usual, rather than to sit for an hour in that spiritual refrigerator. Such prayer-meetings are, we trust, seldom found now, for with the increased interest in the Sabbath-school, the weekly meeting has been steadily growing in importance, in the estimation of Christians of all denominations.

Now, upon whom shall we lay the blame for a lifeless prayer meeting? The safest course is to distribute it all around, for usually pastor and church members are all at fault – the pastor for a lack of preparation, the people for a lack of co-operation. By lack of preparation we do not mean as regards careful thought upon the chapter to be read, for we hold most firmly that one of the chilling influences in such a meeting is the lengthy and elaborate "opening" by the pastor, leaving nothing for the brethren to say, and dampening all enthusiasm to speak. The pastor should simply open the meeting, and read the chapter, saying nothing, unless it be a single thought to give direction to the thoughts of others. His remarks will come in better at the close, when he can occupy five minutes in gathering up the suggestions which have been uttered, and, perhaps, add one or more practical lessons not mentioned by others.

Then the pastor's opening remarks are apt to be more theological than experimental, and they serve to seal the lips of those whose theological education may be deficient, but whose experience of the preciousness of Christ may be very rich.

Then again, the pastor has an opportunity twice on the Sabbath to instruct the church on theological truths, but the prayer-meeting belongs particularly to the people, – it is *their* hour, not *his*, and therefore, it is stealing from them their property, when one-half of the time is occupied by the pastor, who should simply lead and control the exercises. But the pastor may prepare for this meeting by a wise selection of two or three persons, to whom he will state the chapter to be read, so that they will be *ready* to speak as soon as he takes his seat, thus avoiding pauses which kill a prayer-meeting, and making sure the interest of the remarks made. It may happen that these selected speakers will have no chance to speak – so much the better – but they will be ready to fill any possible gap, and their earnest words will kindle an inspiration in other hearts, and will open other lips. In this selection, the same persons should not be often called on; and there should be a difference of age between them, so that the young, as well as the older, will feel that the pastor looks to them for the support of the meeting. The wisdom of such a course will be apparent when we remember that our business men come to the evening meeting from the cares and anxieties of the counting-room, and it can hardly be expected that they will be ready to speak at once on spiritual matters, unless they have been able to prepare their minds by a knowledge of the passage to be read.

Then, in regard to the exercises of the hour, we often err in, running our prayer-meetings in a stereotyped form, so that they become dry and uninteresting – the same thing week after week. There should be plenty of singing, – not an entire hymn, but a verse thrown in between the prayers and remarks. Our people love to sing, and while but few may be able to speak, all can praise God in song. Dispense with the instrument, if possible, but if it is used, do not let precious moments be occupied by playing the melody all through, or by interludes, which are always a serious infliction on the people. Insist that the remarks be very brief, not more than three minutes, and if the brother is burdened to say more, let him keep it carefully for another time. Three minutes are long enough for the utterance of one thought, and this is all that any one person should give in a meeting of only one hour's duration. Have more praying than talking. Many a so-called prayer-meeting is no *prayer*-meeting at all, but is all talk, talk, talk – and it is no wonder they are dull and powerless. The purpose of these gatherings of the church is to gain spiritual strength, and prayer is the grand channel through which this strength can be received; and, therefore, make the hour *full of prayer* – *short* prayers, earnest, simple prayers, but a great many of them. But we are exceeding the limits of an introductory article, and close with urging upon all who love the Church of Christ, and desire its spiritual health and purity and power, to love the prayer-meeting, to seek its increasing interest, so that it shall be the grand spiritual armory of believers, and the very gate of heaven to many, many souls.

May this little book have a blessed mission among the churches!

A. E. Kittredge.

Chapter 1

The Prayer Meeting as a Subject of Study

How to improve the prayer-meeting may not seem so serious a question to our large and prosperous city churches. Evidently it is easier for them to conduct the meetings to general satisfaction and edification than for some of the smaller country churches. They have a membership running up to many hundreds and out of that number many who are fluent speakers, both by culture and profession, whilst in the country the conditions are less favorable, both because the membership is often below a hundred and because there are not in that number more than half a dozen who are in the habit of taking part in the exercises of the meeting. Now, under such circumstances, the charge and improvement of the prayer-meeting becomes a serious question.

It is almost an adage that the successful prayer-meeting will make the successful church and it is equally true that if the prayer-meeting is not a success, it can be made so. There are principles which apply to its conduct, just as well as to successful business or school-keeping. As a matter of course, I would look for no success which is not connected with the Bible and with Bible methods and which does not depend upon the Holy Spirit for its inspiration.

It may be true also that the precise method which would insure success to one church might not, without some modification, do the same for another. There are differences in culture between different congregations. But whatever the method pursued, it should be such that, while it is continuously improving the prayer-meeting, it shall at the same time improve the intellectual and spiritual condition of the church.

The prayer-meeting is all too generally a place to which many laymen go "with fear and trembling." With many it is a comfortless thing for all the time they are afraid that their pastor will see them and call upon them: "Well, Brother Blank, how is it with you? I hope you will testify. Haven't you got a word to say?" Or, "Will you not lead us in prayer?" I think I know why there are more women who attend prayer-meetings than men. They are not required to speak and for them, doubtless, there is peace and comfort in the exercises. I have known men who have sat through a prayer-meeting in a sort of cold chill, with nerves unstrung, wishing the minister would omit them, looking solemn and anxious, until the benediction descended upon them with a joy almost indescribable. There are men so constituted that a call upon them to speak or pray seems to send every idea they ever had to the four quarters of the compass and when, in obedience to the call, they do arise, though it be the coldest kind of weather, the sweat starts and runs in rivulets. "Why, sir," said one of the best men in the world, "If I was to undertake to repeat the Lord's Prayer when called upon in meeting, I don't think I could do it and yet I know it as well as my own name." A man of a very nervous and sensitive temperament would almost as soon have a tooth pulled as to attend a prayer-meeting and sit through the terrible ordeal. When men of this class are regular attendants, their presence is more a duty than a pleasure.

Nor is it anything against a man that may be bashful, timid, or unused to public speaking if his first trials should prove failures. There have been able men and profound thinkers who have been unable to think and speak fluently before an audience. Indeed, it is a matter of history that some of the most brilliant orators in their "maiden speeches" have completely failed.

And, besides, there is another thing to be borne in mind and that is this: the public does not have the same knowledge of our mental states that we ourselves possess. Some men judge of the effect of their remarks or prayers by their own feelings and because these are depressed, they think they cannot speak to edification and so had better keep still. Their thoughts while they are on their feet seem to be flying about in utter confusion, like flakes in a snow-storm, and they feel that others must be as painfully conscious of their agitation as they themselves have been.

How, then, can we assist such men as these to take part with greater pleasure to themselves and profit to others? How can we assure the timid that practice will eventually confirm their nerves and give them a more orderly command of their thoughts while upon their feet and in the presence of the terrifying audience? How can we conduct the meetings so as to make them comfortable for all and cause them to abound in spiritual refreshment and Christian fellowship? How can we discover just the method for our particular charges that will wake up the mind of all the membership and stimulate Bible reading and research, as well as stir up their zeal to renewed activity in all departments of Christian work? How can we make available for righteousness and the good of the church just such talent as our members now possess? How can we secure the attendance of all the membership for the prayer-meeting? In a word, how can we make our prayer-meeting "The Model Prayer-Meeting"?

The cause of Christ and the welfare of the church at large emphasize these and related questions. They demand from every minister that he make their solution the subject of special study and the improvement of the prayer-meeting a matter of prayerful and untiring endeavor. The following pages are offered as a series of hints in this direction.

Chapter 2

The People's Meeting

The prayer-meeting on some evening of the week is the people's meeting. The Sabbath is the day for the ministration of the pastor. They each have their day. If it is not wise for the people to conduct the services of the Sabbath, neither is it wise for the pastor to monopolize the exercises of the week-day meeting. If it is true that the active piety of a church rises no higher than it manifests itself in the prayer-meeting so that here, as on a barometer, all changes in spiritual life are faithfully recorded, then certainly too much attention cannot be given by both pastor and people to the conduct of the prayer-meeting.

The people need just such a meeting as the weekday meeting is, and ought to be, and what it can be made to be, if it is not already. There is so little place given in our churches on Sunday for the participation of the people in its services and, hence, so many have come to regard the day as an entertainment in eloquence and music. If these are wanting, if they cannot hear a fine sermon from one end of the church and be soothed by sweet music from the other, they will not go to church – no, not they. But offer them a lecture and a concert agreeably combined and they may consent to go. Where this idea prevails, the people have forgotten that on Sunday they are to publicly appear before God, to render unto Him worship, prayer, praise and thanksgiving, with confession of their sins, thankful acknowledgment of His mercies, and earnest supplication for new supplies of grace. And all this they can do, though the sermon be never so feeble and the singing never so poor. Have they not forgotten God's promise: "*In all places where I record my name, I will come unto thee, and I will bless thee.*" (Ex. 20:24)? But the people need a meeting in which to tell their experience, comfort one another, pray for one another, and, where the case requires it, bear one another's burdens. Life in the market and the domestic circle, in the shop and the store, in the kitchen and the school-room, in the street and the field, at home and abroad, has its trials and burdens, its anxieties and sorrows, its temptations and defeats, as well as its joys and triumphs. Griefs are lessened and joys are multiplied when others share them with us.

> "Thoughts shut up want air,
> And spoil, like bales unopened to the sun."

How precious, then, is the privilege that admits the Christian to the circle of congenial friends and steadfast companions on the road from earth to heaven. Here they meet to "*Rejoice with them that do rejoice, and weep with them that weep.*" (Rom. 12:15) and so, by mutual vows and endeavors and sympathies, fainting hearts are made resolute, and the tread of uncertain feet firm and victorious.

> "As bees mix'd nectar drawn from fragrant flow'rs,
> So men from friendship, wisdom and delight."

How eagerly the fainting Israelite gathered the freshly-fallen manna! With what alacrity did not the thirsty tribes bound forward as the majestic palm-trees arose before them in the distance – seventy palm-trees, as they clustered around the twelve springs of Elim (Ex. 15:27) and fed their roots from these living fountains – how joyously, we may imagine, did not the air resound with their shouts of "Water! Water! There is water at the roots of the palm-trees!" When the traveler is about to sink beneath the heat and the thirst of his journey through the arid wastes, he sees just before him the green oasis and starts forward with renewed hope to reach its shade and refreshment. When the summer's heat is oppressive and to breathe is burdensome, how gladly mankind seeks the cooling beach of lake or sea, or the green swards, the cooling glens, and the shady trees, rich in leaf and fruit, as these may be found amid the lawn, the field, and the forest.

Ought not the prayer-meeting on the midday of the week to be all this to the Christian who, having set his face Zion-ward, is making the journey to the celestial city; yes, more than all this to him whose feet cannot rest till they walk in safety your golden streets, O Jerusalem! Ought not the prayer-meeting to be the tree with fruit and foliage, the common on which feet are cooled as they walk and sink into the grassy carpet, the oasis with its refreshment, Elim with its seventy palm-trees and twelve fountains of water that never run dry, the company of friends where words may be opened to the sun, where criticism shall be disarmed, and what we desire to say shall be better understood than what we do say, if for any reason our words have proved inadequate?

And just an instance to show what freedom and friendliness characterize the prayer circle may not be out of place here. Not long ago I attended a prayer-meeting in Chicago. Both pastor and people were strangers to me. As the meeting was nearing its close, a convert got up to speak. He was full of love and zeal, as all converts are, but he was evidently unused to public speaking. His hands were kept flying constantly and all about his head, as if fighting an imaginary wasp's nest, whilst his body kept bobbing up and down all the time in a ludicrous manner. Most certainly he satisfied that rule of eloquence which makes it consist in a threefold action and besides all this, his English was quite broken and so rapidly spoken that it was difficult to catch word and sense. Did they laugh? Not exactly; a smile or two may have been suppressed but that was all. Anywhere else he would have been greeted with uproarious laughter. Here however, he secured our pity and we felt more like encouraging him than to dissuade him from his efforts altogether. It is more fit that criticism should sleep in the prayer circle than the members. Whoever feels called upon to pray or speak may do so in the feeling that all will be kindly received and that nothing but generous sympathy awaits him.

The prayer-meeting, then, is the people's meeting and they support its exercises. Here they witness for Christ; here they renew their consecration; here is the place where much good may be done and much good received by words of encouragement and sympathy; and as such the people should relish its opportunities and not neglect its privileges. Had not Thomas been absent from just one meeting of the disciples, he would have received, eight days earlier than he did, the proof he required to save him from skepticism; and had he absented himself continuously, he might have died in unbelief. (John 20:26-29)

People are to put themselves in the way of receiving the blessings of God, for the church in its ordinances is the channel of grace and our spiritual wants will be best ministered unto when we are most constant in our attendance upon all the meetings. And it may prove in our case, as in that of Thomas, that the meetings we miss are the very ones which contain the thoughts, the prayers, the songs, and the experiences for lack of which our souls are famishing, and we are subjected to those temptations which weaken rather than confirm our faith.

> "I've found a glad hosanna
>   For every woe and wail;
> A handful of sweet manna
>   When grapes of Eshcol fail;
> I've found a Rock of Ages
>   When desert wells are dry;
> And after weary stages,
>   I've found an Elim nigh.
>
> My Saviour, Thee possessing,
>   I have found the joy, the balm,
> The healing and the blessing,
>   The sunshine and the psalm;
> The promise for the fearful,
>   The Elim for the faint;
> The rainbow for the tearful.
>   The glory for the saint!"

Chapter 3

Preparation

The pastor does not presume to enter the pulpit Sabbath after Sabbath without proper preparation. He has a very low view of his duty, the dignity of the pulpit, as well as of the privilege and pleasure of preaching who thinks anything is good enough for the pulpit and is willing to rush before his people, as the horse to battle, with stray scraps of thought. When Dr. Beecher once preached to the students of Andover and was asked how long it took him to prepare that sermon, he replied in his peculiar way, "Twenty years." The full sermon comes from the full preparation and years of study behind it.

The pastor cannot rely upon inspiration to take the place of study, nor look for a miracle to supply him text and thought at the time he is to preach. It is true that the disciples were to take no thought as to what they should say when brought before magistrates, for in the same hour they should be told what to say (Luke 12:11-12). Emergencies and exceptional cases will often arise when the preacher will have to rely upon God for his sermon entirely and then the sermon comes to him, not as a substitute for his fidelity but in connection with it, and more will be accomplished by it than by that which could have been premeditated. At one of the places in which C. G. Finney was holding revival services, an infidel club was formed, it is said, for the purpose of opposing Christian work. The leader was a physician, who, on one occasion, slipped into the church and seated himself in the choir. Mr. Finney coming in and, as usual, glancing about his audience, saw this man and at once changed his text and preached that morning a powerful sermon on the plan of salvation, taking as his text: *"For God so loved the world that He gave His only-begotten Son that whosoever believeth in Him should not perish, but have everlasting life."* (John 3:16). In the afternoon, the doctor came again and the sermon on the text *"How shall we escape if we neglect so great salvation?"* (Heb. 2:3) seemed to be the logical sequence of the morning's sermon. In the evening, the doctor was again present and the sermon was a conclusion of the whole matter from the text, *"But they made light of it"* (Matt. 22:5). A lady spoke to the doctor at the close of the service: "Doctor, you've heard the truth; now, are you going away tonight to make light of it?"

"No, ma'am, I am not," was his reply. That night he tried to sleep but at midnight he rose and paced the room until he cried to his wife: "Wife, I can't live so, and I won't live so."

Now, as Mr. Finney was in the habit of going from place to place to labor as an evangelist, he no doubt had a number of sermons prepared for this especial work and the inference is a fair one that these sermons had the practical connection which study and perhaps previous use had given them and, having many arrows in his quiver, he would naturally select those that would be best adapted to reach certain persons in his audience when he knew them to be present.

The example of the disciples is exceptional, of course, for they had a particular promise to rely upon. In their missionary labors they would encounter dangers and difficulties too great for human prudence and premeditation to remove. Therefore the promise of the Holy Spirit to assist them gave peace and quiet to their minds and sent them forward on their labors with hope and courage. God will supply all need in the hour of emergency—*"for without Me ye can do nothing."* (John 15:5) – but God does not promise to do for us what He designs we should do for ourselves. As relates to diligence, study, and preparation, all human need is well expressed in that Cromwellian motto, "Trust in God, but keep your powder dry."

But as the prayer-meeting, in the main, is the people's meeting, it is hardly necessary to ask if they need preparation for its exercises. And to give this pointed application, we may ask ourselves, "For what purpose do we attend the prayer-meeting?" When we clearly understand its object, we shall better see to what extent preparation is necessary.

This meeting is needed in order that the religious life of the church may find public expression by the people themselves. Soldiers come together that they may drill and perfect themselves in the manual of arms. Soldiers who cannot execute the commands of the officer with alacrity and uniformity would make a sorry army and earn but little headway against an enemy well-officered and in a state of splendid discipline. The people should come together that like comrades they may stand shoulder to shoulder. By the expression of their trials and victories, their confessions and their aspirations, and their words of prayer and praise, they may go through the exercises of the spiritual manual. They learn how good a thing fellowship is and what a blessed privilege the communion of saints forms for the disciple here below. And in thus sharing their experiences of joy and sorrow, of faith, hope and love, they may learn the better to keep step together in the Christian life and make their conflict with the world, the flesh, and the devil more victorious.

The people need this meeting as an aid to growth in grace. The experience of every Christian will show that his seasons of most rapid progress in the Christian walk and in the attainment of the Christian graces coincide with the seasons when he was faithful in the use of his resources, regular in attendance upon the ordinances of God's house and the prayer-meeting, and when his voice was lifted up to praise God in company with his brethren. Times of backsliding and lukewarm indifference will be found to have been those in which he neglected the means of grace and when what he considered of more importance kept him from the prayer-meeting. Guerilla warfare does not equal that service which is regular and systematic.

The people need the prayer-meeting for the cultivation of the devotional spirit. Songs of praise acquire a power when tuned by many voices and especially so if they are sung with the spirit and the understanding. Words of prayer, however simple, if heartfelt, possess a reflex influence and a new power from the assenting presence of the brethren. When "amen," either audibly or silently, is added to the prayer, it becomes the prayer of all and receives force from that very circumstance. God does not judge the prayer by the graces of rhetoric and the rules of grammar but by its faith and sincerity. *"Likewise the Spirit also helpeth our infirmities: for we know not what we should pray for as we ought; but the Spirit itself maketh intercession for us with groanings which cannot be uttered."* (Rom. 8:26). Words without heart in them, however eloquent otherwise, never find their way to heaven but rise about as high as the head. We are blessed in the attendance of those meetings which are marked by the absence of formal praise and stilted prayers; our faith is confirmed, our love is warmed, our hope is encouraged, and our whole life is progressively sanctified thereby. From such meetings, where our hearts have melted under divine love, where our souls have been refreshed with heavenly manna and water flowing from the living Rock, one does not think of rushing to places of frivolity and worldly amusement.

When Moses was coming down from the mount where he had communed with God during forty days and the wicked and thoughtless frivolity and idolatry of his people met his gaze, his soul was filled with righteous indignation and the two tables of stone were dashed in pieces at his feet (Ex. 32:19, Dt. 9:17). The contrast was too great and too sudden – communion with God in its power and sweetness on the one hand and gross superstition and naked idolatry on the other.

The people need the prayer-meeting that they may have an opportunity, in the spirit of Hebrews 10:24-25, to study each other with special reference to temperament and peculiarities and that they may be able to more readily provoke each other unto love and to good works. Such provocation as shall make the fruit of the Spirit grow and ripen is not only permissible but even commendable. The Christian is to regard his brethren as textbooks for study, with the view of constantly improving them in the nurture of every needed grace and virtue.

And if the pastor should ask, how can I do more than I am already doing, it might be suggested that he give a whole day to planning and preparing for each meeting. Monday is generally considered a "blue" day with ministers. It would seem that this day might be turned to good account in many ways. Suppose he spend this day in visiting his people and following up a little the impressions produced by his Sabbath ministrations. He would receive many a stimulating word and suggestion that would help him in his work for the next Sabbath and while the iron is thus hot, he might make some good hits for the coming prayer-meeting and get a limited number to promise and come especially prepared with reference to a given topic. As he visits from house to house, special cases of spiritual need and sympathy will arise; formulate such cases as these and make each one the topic for special prayer. Ask someone to come and pray for one who may be sick; another one to pray for one peculiarly tempted; another to pray for himself that he may receive grace and strength to labor for the salvation of some friend with whom he may have especial influence. In this way not only particular areas of need in a congregation will be prayed for and doubtless with the most beneficial results but also new topics for special prayer will constantly arise to keep pace with the steady and healthy growth in grace of the whole church and enlarge the sphere of its influence and usefulness.

And I would suggest for trial that the execution of a plan for each meeting be entrusted to a committee of two or three ladies who make it their duty to see those whom the pastor desires to take part in a particular meeting; and, in case those designated cannot serve, to secure substitutes and then to visit the parish with the expressed object of securing a full attendance upon the meeting and creating by anticipation an interest in its exercises. The entire lady membership of the church might be successively employed in this way. Nor would it prove for them an arduous duty inasmuch as each one would not be called upon to serve more than once or twice a year. Nor again should it dispense with as full a pastoral visitation as possible in connection with each meeting for it is evident to all that a co-operation of this kind would not only give the ladies congenial employment but also serve to get everybody in the church interested in the prayer-meeting. And if it should result in a generous rivalry on their part as to which meeting shall become the most profitable and refreshing, the prayer-meeting would lose nothing by such wholesome zeal. In this way, too, the ladies would begin to feel that they are taking a most important part in the meeting even though they remain silent.

Finally, let each one that the pastor asks to take a part come early to the meeting and as soon as he gets a chance, after the introductory services, arise and pray or offer remarks. In this way there will be a rapid movement in the meeting like the tramp of an army on the march and a progress something like that which characterizes the Gospel of St. Mark, who takes us from *"The beginning of the Gospel of Jesus Christ"* (Mark 1:1) on until *"The Lord was received up into heaven,"* (Mark 16:19) in sixteen chapters. Upon such a church as this – a church realizing that it is *"Not by might, nor by power, but by my Spirit"* (Zech. 4:6) and earnestly seeking to know the mind of the Spirit – God will bestow, according to His promise, a burden of prayer and guide it into such a path of success as shall keep it in constant revival.

Now it may be that prayer-meetings are not more largely attended and more generally successful because both pastor and people allow them to take care of themselves with the feeling that the odds and ends of thought – the apple-parings and peach-stones – gathered from second-hand experience will be good enough for the week-day meeting. Life, experience, and the best thoughts from the history which each one is writing of himself is what we want for the prayer-meeting and such songs as shall express our faith, love, and aspiration. If this field is to bear a large harvest, it must be faithfully worked. He who spends the most time in the cultivation of his farm, who uses the best seed with a liberal sowing, is the one that secures the best harvest and the largest income. Weeds are about the only things that need no cultivation.

Chapter 4

The Daily Cultivation of Piety

There are some who seem to hate religion. They will not enter the Kingdom themselves nor permit others to enter it, if they can prevent it by their words and opposition. There are some who seem indifferent about religion. It does not matter to them, one way or another, whether Christianity is true or false. Life in the present is so busy and so full of cares that if they can only make a living now, they will let the life in the hereafter take care of itself. They will run their chances. There are some who have a great respect for religion. They give liberally to the support of the Gospel. If their children are converted and unite with the church, they are glad. They know their children will grow up to be better men and women if they become religious. Such are like "Noah's carpenters" – they help to build the ark but neglect to enter it themselves. Some are willing that their wives be religious but their own case is such that they cannot attend to religion just now. They are in pursuit of wealth, or pleasure, or ambition. If they should become religious, it would require a change in their business; or if not that, at least a change in the manner of conducting it. For the present, you must have them excused. When they have a convenient season they will send for you (Acts 24:25).

There are others who profess religion but do not prosecute it with any zeal. Their religion is for Sunday. They attend church regularly but when the doors of the church are closed, their hearts are closed also and during the week they give themselves up to the worldly spirit. There are others who add company religion to this Sunday religion. Such are not anxious to entertain ministers or earnest Christians at their homes during the holding of religious meetings and conventions because this requires of them that they should have family worship morning and evening. But they are hospitable and so, for the time being, they dust their Bibles, oil their knees, and kindle a fire upon the family altar. And there are others, also, whose religion is a proxy religion. They are reverential; they daily bend the knees at family worship and are constant in attendance upon all the ordinances of God's house but they never pray themselves. Others do the praying for them in the family, in the prayer-meeting, and in the church. They may silently or audibly say "Amen," but as for themselves, they neither pray in public, in private, nor in secret. They are prayer-less Christians.

Why is it that religion is not relished more than appears to be the case? Why, in so many cases, is it that Christian life is so feeble? Is it because religion has come to be merely professional? Let a physician be called and, though he be ever so kind and gentle, yet he is apt from long practice to look at the patient and his disease from a professional standpoint rather than enter fully into sympathy with him as a man and a brother.

During the late civil war it became my opportunity, as a member of the Sanitary Commission, to attend upon some wounded soldiers as they were being taken by steamboat from White House Landing, VA, to Washington. There were some fifteen of us to take care of 405 men. Two surgeons of the regular army accompanied us. I became greatly interested in the case of a poor fellow whose wound was in a bad condition and needed skillful and instant attention. I endeavored to get one of the doctors to do something for him. He came and after making some experiments to ascertain the extent of the injury, he said that he could do nothing for him as he was in need of a particular instrument. "You must wait till you get to Washington." Now there was something in the manner so heartless and indifferent that I was astonished and yet I have no right to suppose that he was an unkind man. He simply viewed the case from the standpoint of his profession. For myself, I could get no sleep during those sixty hours that we were on that boat. We who had volunteered to take care of those men felt their sufferings to be a terrible strain upon our nervous system. We were unused to such sights and sufferings and the amount of sympathy called for was almost more than we could endure.

Now, it may be that something like this takes place in our religious experience. After a while we lose its early fervor. Our religion ceases to be new, fresh, emotional, and inspirational; it becomes professional. I remember during a revival at college when I first began to feel the new life in its preciousness – in its fullness of promise, hope, and inheritance – how near the Saviour seemed to be. As I was going to my room after one of the evening meetings, everything appeared to be new. "*Old things are passed away; behold all things are become new.*" (2 Cor. 5:17). It was a lovely evening. I looked up into the sky, and the stars were twinkling with a friendly luster I had never noticed before. The thought that all these things are mine because I am His, took possession of my soul. "*All are yours; and ye are Christ's, and Christ is God's.*" (1 Cor. 3:22-23). If the child of nature in a moment of enthusiasm can say, as he looks up at the sun, its rays glittering from the leaves of the overarching trees in the grove, "This is my air, my sunshine, my earth," how much more truly may not the child of God, as he beholds the works of his Father's hand, exclaim," My air, my sunshine, my earth!"

Now, how can we return to a state like this of tender susceptibility if we have lost it? I can never forget how deeply I was impressed during my school days by the example of a devout Christian whose heart seemed so full of love, that he never could mention the name of the Savior without a tear starting from his eyes and his lips quivering with emotion. How can we live so as to enjoy religion every hour of the day? Can the answer be otherwise than by the daily and careful cultivation of piety? Set apart half an hour every day for secret prayer and the devotional study of God's Word. An hour at a time would not be too much and half an hour will not be too little; but when the half-hour becomes a habit, the season will prove so precious and be found so necessary to the support of Christian life that the full hour will be approximated and such daily custom will prevent the religious life from becoming merely professional or a wearisome duty.

Seek to be alone at such a time; "When thou prayest, enter into thy closet, and when thou hast shut thy door, pray to thy Father, which is in secret; and thy Father which seeth in secret shall reward thee openly." (Matt. 6:6) And let it be the first half-hour in the day for "The morning hour has gold in its mouth." Let the first half-hour of the day before food, before family, before daily avocation be made sacred to the Lord.

God has given us three most valuable gifts – His Word, His Son, and His Spirit. We need to study the Word because the Holy Spirit uses that as an instrument to communicate God's Will, to convince and convert, and to edify and sanctify our *"whole spirit, and soul and body"* (1 Thess. 5:23). The Holy Spirit glorifies Christ in the Word. We need to study it, therefore, and to pray over it. God is the object of our worship, Christ is the basis of our worship, the Holy Spirit is the agency of our worship – our Guide, Teacher and Comforter, and the Word is the Instrument. And so the Word of God will furnish holy themes for the "secret hour," which, like fuel cast upon fire, shall feed the flame of devotion and cause it to glow with a steady light.

And now the practice of spending such a season – the first moments of the day – in secret prayer and communion with God has been a habit with many prominent men and devoted Christians.

"It is said [that] of one of our most eminent statesmen," observes Dr. Murphy, "at a time when most responsible duties to the country rested on him, that his morning hour was always spent in imploring the help of the Great Ruler of the Nations. A distinguished judge acknowledged his success in his profession as owing to the hour he daily spent with God. General Havelock, though burdened with the care of the army during the terrible mutiny in India, managed to keep sacred for prayer a long time in the morning of each day. Other names might be added, as those of Bacon and the great astronomer Kepler and the historian De Thou, of whom it is related, every morning he implored God in private to purify his heart, to banish from it hatred and flattery, to enlighten his mind, and to make known to him the truth which so many passions and conflicting interests had almost buried. This was also the custom of one, guided by the Holy Spirit, for David's resolution was: *'My voice shalt thou hear in the morning, O Lord; in the morning will I direct my prayer unto thee, and will look up.'* (Ps. 5:3). The testimony of that most godly man, Philip Henry, speaking of one of his studying days, was: 'I forgot, when I began, explicitly and expressly to crave help from God and the chariot-wheels drove accordingly. Lord forgive my omission, and keep me in the way of duty!' What higher example and encouragement could we have for this practice?"

And there are those who do not find the morning season sufficient for the daily wants of the spiritual life after such a practice has once become fixed. In the Methodist Church Block in Chicago, before the great fire, "[t]here was a certain dark closet under a stairway, used for the storage of wood and coal," which, as every other nook and corner of the building was occupied, Moody and his earnest co-laborers used as a closet for secret prayer. There, alone or in company, these devout Christians used to shut themselves up and while the great business world rolled around them above and below, like the sea around Jonah, they held sweet communion with their Lord. Charles G. Finney states in his autobiography (Finney, 1908) that he discovered, while a guest in the house of Anson G. Phelps, that this distinguished merchant of New York was in the habit of arising in the night, after having taken a nap, to secretly hold communion with his God. *"Seven times a day do I praise thee"* (Ps. 119:164), says the sweet singer of Israel. Three times a day did Daniel kneel in his chamber with his *"windows being open . . . toward Jerusalem"* (Dan. 6:10). Sir Thomas Browne wrote in his journal as an admonition to himself, "To be sure to let no day pass without calling upon God in a solemn-formed prayer seven times within the compass thereof: that is, in the morning and at night and five times between."

Secret prayer has a transforming influence. *"As he prayed, the fashion of his countenance was altered, and his raiment was white and glistering."* (Luke 9:29). Through the Spirit of God, by its refining power, the human spirit is changed into the image of Christ from glory to glory. And even the body is ennobled by the daily habit of rapt communion with God. A flame from heaven descends upon the intellect, divine warmth cheers the heart, a gentle sunshine irradiates the brow, and upon every feature the Heavenly Dove doth seem to brood.

> There is no power like secret prayer to make
> The fleshly garment from the Spirit take
> Its shape and look. The pure soul will transform
> The poorest tabernacle – 'tis life's norm –

> And cause beyond the fuller's power to glow,
> As on the Mount, and glister like the snow.
> No other action so can beautify
> And give to man a grace that shall not die,
> As this of daily meeting with our Lord
> In faith and love to feed upon His Word.

Be sure then to begin the day aright and from such daily cultivation of piety and the devotional spirit, shall come the best preparation for all the active duties of life. By such a habit the heart will be kept in tune for every religious duty and from its practice will grow such a relish for the services of the prayer-meeting as shall make the more special preparation for its exercises a joy and not an annoying burden.

> "More holiness give me,
>   More strivings within;
> More patience in suff'ring,
>   More sorrow for sin;
> More faith in my Savior,
>   More sense of His care!
> More joy in His service,
>   More purpose in prayer."

Chapter 5

The Topics

But in addition to all this, it will be well to have a topic for each meeting with reference to which the people, as well as the pastor, may make special preparation. It should be our endeavor to make each meeting new, fresh, and stimulating; both helpful and hopeful. Prayer-meetings have come to be so proverbially "stale, flat, and unprofitable," because the excellent brethren who take part week in and year out repeat over and over the same remarks and the same prayers. The daily cultivation of piety will give depth and flavor to prayer and the religious life and a given topic previously announced will afford the people an opportunity to arrange their thoughts with reference to it and to select such things from their experience as shall illustrate the topic in an interesting manner and on the principle of unity. When the people assemble in ignorance of the subject and the line of thought to be presented, it is not to be looked for that all parts shall fit into their place and produce a deep and abiding impression, or, indeed, that they shall speak at all to edification and to the point. Lord Nelson had a carefully prepared plan for the battle of Trafalgar in which each ship had its place assigned in the line of action and all together were so massed that they should form a wedge and sweep right through the ranks of the enemy. As he planned, so it proved. The victory was decisive and placed him in the front rank of great naval heroes. When the exercises are so arranged that they have plan and unity; when the chapter has been read, the hymns sung, the remarks made, and the prayers offered are so directed that they illustrate the given topic and the special needs of the church, each part will take its place in the line to form the wedge and no one will be able to go away and say the meeting lacked purpose, point, and power.

Nor will it be found an easy matter to select just the right kind of topics for the prayer-meeting. It would not be surprising if ministers spent as much time over this as over selecting the subject and text for their sermons. In order to avoid this difficulty and the loss of time, many have chosen the topics of the Sunday-school lesson and made them the basis of their remarks. Much might be said in favor of this. It has the advantage of system and publicity and so gives opportunity to others beside the minister to make intelligent remarks upon the subject. Speech, to be most profitable, needs to be premeditated as to the substance of thought. Where both words and thought are spontaneous, unless the man is inspired by the Spirit of the Lord for the occasion, it will be just as well if he kept silent.

But the Sunday-school topics are selected more with reference to the wants of a school than the needs of a prayer-meeting and daily Christian life. If there is a general attendance on the prayer-meeting and the Sunday-school – as is desirable – it takes away from the freshness of the theme and the interest in it also to have the same topic presented twice and, in connection with the teachers' meeting, thrice in the same week. The topics more especially needed for the week-day meeting are such as grow out of the trials and burdens of daily life and should be so adapted to them as to confer sympathy, bestow strength and patience, and promote growth in grace. The prayer-meeting should give scope for such themes as are particularly adapted to edify the body of Christ, to confirm faith, to quicken love, to illustrate doctrine, and to stimulate life in its various fields of useful labor. Hence the more appropriate themes are such as make plain our duty to God, to self, and to fellow-man. The topics should be selected with reference to the guidance of experience along *"the path of the just,"* which *"is as the shining light, that shineth more and more unto the perfect day."* (Prov. 4:18).

And topics might also be selected occasionally to bear some relevancy to the progress of time and the changing seasons. Thus, for a New Year's week we might have a dedication service on some such theme as this, *"Choose you this day whom ye will serve"* (Josh. 24:15), or "Mary's Choice" (Luke 10:38-42).

For a spring service, we might choose a topic like this, "Seed Time" (Gal. 6:7), or we might arrange for a "Floral Service" just as spring is passing into summer and is now standing in its pride and glory – *"Consider the lilies of the field, how they grow"* (Matt. 6:28). Services of this kind would teach valuable lessons as well as give suitable opportunity to pray for a blessing upon the sowing of the seed and the increase of the material harvest in its season.

A promise meeting might be arranged for some time during the progress of summer and opportunity given for rehearsing the promises of God and their unfailing fulfillment in our experience.

A "harvest festival" would be appropriate for the autumn and the ingathering of grain and fruit. These would find their counterpart in the reaping of life's spiritual harvest (2 Cor. 9:6 and Gal. 6:7-9). Themes of a kindred nature would be: "The Summer is Ended," (Jer. 8:20) "Fruits Meet for Repentance," (Matt. 3:8) "The Fruit of the Holy Spirit," (Gal.5:22-23) "The Fruit of the Lips," (Isa. 57:19) etc.

On Thanksgiving week, it would be very appropriate to have a general praise meeting in which the people may express what they have to be thankful for and such a meeting on their part would prove a most excellent preparation for the public observance of the day of Thanksgiving.

And for the close of the year we might have a remembrance meeting: *"Hitherto hath the Lord helped us."* (1 Sam. 7:12). It would be very profitable to review the signal providences of the year and apply the teachings of age to renewed faithfulness for time is short and its flight rapid. Would not such a meeting as this deepen our appreciation of the 90th psalm and especially that devout petition, *"So teach us to number our days, that we may apply our hearts unto wisdom."*? (Psalm 90:12) Topic would suggest topic as the seasons come and go and in this way we could appropriately arrange for evenings in which to illustrate the various teachings of nature as they bear upon life. We should find occasions in this way to use the great phenomena of nature and use them as the Bible uses them, to illustrate life and its meanings. In this way mountain, river, sea, storm, wind, rain, dew, ice, and snow could be used for the topics at such times as would render them appropriate but not so frequently as to destroy freshness and render their teachings trite and distasteful.

And this matter of set topics has already had the trial of years and has been found most expedient by those churches which have used them. There is before me among others the list that was used by the Second Presbyterian Church of Indianapolis, IN, during the last year of the pastorate of Dr. J. L. Withrow. We insert it at the close of this chapter both to commend the method and to show the nature of the topics, that in this way our hints may have the benefit of example as well as precept.

TOPICS

Date	Topic	Reference
Jan. 6	Daily Benefits	Psalms 68:19
13	Suffering Due to Sin	John 5:5
20	Refusing and the Results	John 5:40
27	Born Again	John 3:3
Feb. 3	Evidences of Sonship	Rom. 8:14
10	Resist the Devil	James 4:7
17	Meaning of	Col. 2:10
24	Retribution	Rom. 2:6
Mar. 2	Sparing Begets Sparseness	2 Cor. 9:6
9	Lying	Col. 3:9
16	God Forgetting Sins	Heb. 10:17
23	Christ in Providence	Heb. 1:3
30	Number of the Blest Unknown	Matt. 14:14
Apr. 6	Inspiration of the Scriptures	2 Tim. 3:16
13	Searching the Scriptures	John 5:39
20	Meaning of	Hab. 2:4
27	Cleansing Blood	1 John 1:7
May 4	The Good Times of the Ungodly	Ps. 73:5
11	Christ the Leader	Is. 55:4
17	The Intercessor	Heb. 7:25
24	Believing All the Bible	John 5:47
June 1	Union of Faith and Everlasting Life	John 6:47
8	Faith Kneeling at His Feet	John 11:32
15	How?	2 Cor. 5:21

22	Meaning of Repentance	Acts 2:38
29	Sublimity of Unselfishness	2 Cor. 12:15
July 6	Genuine Love	1 John 3:18
13	The Sin-Bearer	1 Pet. 2:24
20	Believing vs. Working	Rom. 4:5
27	The Living Fountain	Rev. 7:17
Aug. 3	Evils of Indulgence	1 Cor. 9:25
10	Refuge from the Storm	Is. 25:4
16	Friend of Friends	Prov. 18:24
23	Explain	Rom. 6:1
30	Saved by Hope	Rom. 8:24
Sept. 7	Putting on Christ	Rom. 13:14
13	Safety	Psalm 91:1
20	All-Seeing Eye	Prov. 15:3
27	Full Satisfaction	Ps. 17:15
Oct. 5	In What Sense?	Rom. 6:18
12	Foolishness of Preaching	1 Cor. 1:18
19	Better than He Asked	2 Cor. 12:9
26	Crowned With Many Crowns	Rev. 19:12
Nov. 2	Consulting Others' Weakness	Rom. 15:1
9	Relation of Believers to the Savior	Col. 2:7
16	Right Kind of Righteousness	Phil. 3:9
23	Thanksgiving	Eph. 5:20
30	Harmonize	Gal. 6:2, 6:5
Dec. 7	Gracious Promise	Mal. 4:2
14	The Unborn Herald	Mal. 4:5
21	The Star	Matt. 2:10
28	The End	Ps. 39:4

Chapter 6

The Topics Illustrated

It will prove quite stimulating and an aid to the fuller understanding of Scriptural truth to draw from the Bible suitable illustrations of the changing seasons and of striking events in the history of our church, our community, our state, or our land as these are providentially unfolded. A few examples have been selected as hints in this direction. And services of this kind in the prayer-meeting will occasionally afford opportunity for an object lesson in decoration. Thus, at Waverly, NY, on the occasion of a harvest sermon by W. H. Bates, the young ladies of the Bible class decorated the church in keeping with the service. Back of the pulpit was placed an evergreen motto, "*Whatsoever a man soweth that shall he also reap.*" (Gal. 6:7). Above it was a sheaf of grain and below an anchor of white immortelles ("everlasting flowers") and evergreen as an emblem of the idea that those who have not come to life's reaping are sowing in immortal hope. The pulpit was festooned with Madeira vines and brilliant autumn leaves. In each corner of the room was a shock of corn and at suitable places were sheaves of ripened grain while upon the communion table were placed two pyramids of apples, pears, peaches, grapes, etc. The sermon was from Psalms 65:11: "*Thou crownest the year with thy goodness.*"

The Opening of the Year (Luke 13:6-9)

In countries where the vine is cultivated, not by a few wealthy proprietors with a view to an export trade but by each family on a small scale with a view to the food of the household, to plant some trees of other kinds within the same enclosure is the rule rather than the exception. Within this favored spot, the owner is willing to make room for one or more fig trees for the sake of the fruit which, in such favorable circumstances, he expects them to bear.

When the tree described in the above passage from Luke 13 had reached maturity, the owner expected that it should bear fruit; but that year, the next, and the third it continued barren. Having waited a reasonable time, he gave orders that it should be destroyed.

The dresser of the vineyard, as is quite natural, had become attached to the tree and when the sentence was pronounced against it, a sentiment akin to compassion springs up. "Woodman, spare that tree," is a kind of intercession thoroughly natural and human. A very significant exemplification of this parable is found in an Arabian receipt for curing a palm tree of barrenness: "Thou must take a hatchet, and go to the tree with a friend, unto whom thou sayest, 'I will cut down the tree, for it is unfruitful.'

"He answers, 'Do not so; this year it will certainly bear.'

"But the other says, 'It must needs be – it must be hewn down' and gives the stem of the tree blows with the back of the hatchet.

"His friend restrains him, crying, 'Nay, do it not; thou wilt certainly have fruit from it this year only have patience and be not over-hasty in cutting it down. If it still refuses to bear fruit, then cut it down.'"

The lesson of this parable is easily read but when read it is unspeakably solemn and tender. God is the owner of the vineyard and the fig tree within its walls. Abraham's seed, natural and spiritual, are the fig tree and the Mediator between God and man is the dresser of the vineyard, the intercessor for the barren tree. The essential circumstances involved in the fact that the fig tree grew within the vineyard are that in soil, south exposure, care, and defense it was placed in the best possible position for bearing fruit. The one fact that it was planted in the vineyard indicates, and was obviously intended to indicate, that the owner had done the best for his fig tree.

The three kinds of works whereof Scripture speaks may all be illustrated from this parable: First, good works (John 6:28; Tit. 2:7), when the tree having been made good bears fruit after its own kind; then dead works (Heb. 9:14; Gal. 2:16), such as have a fair outward appearance but are not the genuine outgrowth of the renewed man – fruit as it were fastened on externally, alms given that they may be gloried in, prayers made that they may be seen, and lastly, wicked works (1 John 3:12; Rom. 13:12; Gal. 5:19-21) when the corrupt tree bears fruit manifestly after its own kind. Here it is that those good fruits are sought but of which none are found. And on that command, "Cut it down," St. Basil beautifully bids us note the love which breathes even in the threatenings of God. "This," he says, "is peculiar to the clemency of God toward men, that He does not bring in punishments silently or secretly; but, by His threatening, first proclaims them to be at hand, thus inviting sinners to repentance." That grand old proverb, which so finely expresses the noiseless approach of the divine judgments, "The gods have feet of wool," while true for others, is not true for those who have a listening ear. Before the hewing down begins, the axe is laid at the root of the tree (Luke 3:9).

Christ, the great Intercessor, desires for men to be saved, yet not that men may always continue unpunished in their sins, but that their sentence may for a while be suspended so to prove whether they will turn and repent. The means of grace shall be multiplied which are so often granted to men and nations in the last period of their probation and just before those means are withdrawn from them forever. Thus before the flood they had Noah, before the great catastrophes of the Jewish people some of their most eminent prophets, and before its final doom, the ministry of Christ and of His apostles. This last is intended for us here; that richer supply of grace, that freer outpouring of the Spirit which should follow on the death, resurrection, and ascension of the Lord. Theophylact says: "Though they were not made better by the law and the prophets, nor yielded fruit or repentance, yet I will water them by my doctrines and passion; it may be that they will then yield fruits of obedience." To us entering upon a new year, the door of repentance and improvement is still left open, *"If it bear fruit, well. If not, how shall we escape, if we neglect so great salvation?"* (Luke 13:9, Heb. 2:3)

– Adapted from Arnot and Trench.

Seed Time – The Sower, the Seed, and the Soil. (Matt. 13:1-9)

This parable represents the reception of the Word of God in the world and presents the causes of failure and the requirements that are necessary in order to secure an abundant and fruitful harvest.

The causes of failure are:

There is a want of spiritual perception. Some of the seed fell by the wayside. There are persons whose religion is all outside – it never penetrates beyond the intellect. Duty is recognized in word, but not felt. They are regular at church, understand the catechism and articles, consider the church a most venerable institution, and have a respect for religion but it never stirs the depths of their being. They feel nothing in it beyond a safeguard for the decencies and respectabilities of social life. Truth of life is subject to failure in such hearts because it is trodden down. Wheat dropped by a harvest cart upon a road, lies outside. There comes a passenger's foot and crushes some of it, then wheels come by – the wheel of traffic and the wheel of pleasure – crushing it grain by grain. And again, the seed finding no place disappears. The fowls of the air come and devour it. This is the picture, not of thought crushed by degrees, but of thought dissipated and no man can tell when or how it went.

There is a want of depth in character. Some fell on stony ground; that is, into a thin layer of soil upon a bed of rock. Shallow soil is like superficial character. You meet such persons in life. There is nothing deep about them; it is all on the surface. The superficial servant's work is done but not thoroughly – lazily, partially.

The superficial workman's labor will not bear inspection. The very dress of such persons betrays the incomplete character of their minds. With such, religion shares the fate of everything else – it is taken up in a superficial way. The seed sprang up quickly and then withered away as quickly because it had no depth of root. There are easily moved susceptibilities that play upon the surface of the soul and then as rapidly pass away. In such persons, words are ever at command – articulate and impassioned words. Such a man came to the Master – running, kneeling, full of warm expressions, engaging gestures, and professed admiration – he was ready for anything. Well, go sell what thou hast. If you wish to know what hollowness and heartlessness are, you must seek for them in the world of light, elegant, superficial fashion where frivolity has turned the heart into a rock bed of selfishness. (Matt. 19:21-22, Mark 10:21-22, Luke 18:22-23).

Impressions come to nothing when the mind is subjected to dissipating influences and yields to them. There are nutrients in the ground for thorns and enough for wheat but not enough in any ground for both wheat and thorns. The heart has a certain power of loving, but love, dissipated on many objects, concentrates itself on none. It must be either God *or* the world, not both. *"No man can serve two masters."* (Matt. 6:24) *"If any man love the world, the love of the Father is not in him."* (1 John 2:15) *"The cares of this world, and the deceitfulness of riches, . . . choke the word!"* (Mark 4:19) There is a way God has of dealing with such which is no pleasant thing to bear. In agriculture it is called weeding and in orchards it is done by pruning.

In the second place, the permanence of religious impressions requires three things:

An honest and good heart is indispensable. Earnestness is necessary for real success in everything. The miser sacrifices all to his single passion, hoards the pennies, and dies possessed of wealth. Time and pains will do anything. *"The kingdom of heaven suffereth violence, and the violent take it by force."* (Matt. 11:12) Sow for time, and probably you will succeed in time. Sow the seed of Life – humbleness, pureheartedness, love, – and in the long eternity which lies before the soul, every minutest grain will come up again with an increase of thirty, sixty, or an hundred fold.

Meditation is necessary. They keep the word which they have heard. In meditation on religious truth, if it be first loved, it will recur spontaneously to the heart. And as it is dwelt on, it receives innumerable applications, is again and again brought up to the sun and tried in various lights, and so incorporates itself with the realities of practical existence. Meditation is done in silence. By it we renounce our narrow individuality and expand into that which is infinite. There is a divine depth in silence – we meet God alone.

Endurance likewise is necessary. *"They bring forth fruit with patience."* (Luke 8:15). The patience for us to cultivate is to bear and to persevere.

However dark and profitless, however painful and weary existence may have become, however any man, like Elijah, may be tempted to cast himself beneath the juniper tree and say, *"It is enough... O Lord!"* (1 Ki. 19:4) Life is not done and our Christian character is not won so long as God has anything left for us to suffer or anything left for us to do. Patience is also opposed to that restlessness which cannot wait. This is one of the difficulties of spiritual life. We are disappointed if the harvest does not come at once.

From all this, it is evident that the causes of failure cannot be attributed to the seed nor to the sower but entirely to the soil.

> "Let us, then, be up and doing,
> With a heart for any fate;
> Still achieving, still pursuing,
> Learn to labor and to wait."
> – *Selected and abridged from Robertson.*

A Summer Service – The Lesson of Flowers. (Matt. 6:28).

We are now almost midway in the season of flowers, between the coming of the early violet and the late chrysanthemum, and are witnessing them in their various phases of bloom, beauty, glory, and rapid decay. Material things are the visible and transient forms into which ideas have been cast and a flower forms one of the many words which God uses in the language of symbolism for lessons of truth and wisdom. We are too apt to think that the material things of earth alone have permanence and reality and serve as the patterns of all thinking and experience but this is the error of materialism. The truth is on the other side. The pattern of things is unseen and eternal. Thoughts are not the fleeting shadows which matter casts; but, more correctly, matter in its various forms is their shadow (2 Cor. 4:18; Col. 2:17; Heb. 8:5 and 9:23).

What, then, are some of the lessons which flowers teach?

From ancient times, the gift of a flower has conveyed the language of esteem and friendship, and in their use on Decoration Day they have come to be emblematical of the affection entertained for those who gave their lives to the service of their country. Flowers form the symbolism of love and beauty, as appears from such popular names as "forget-me-not," "love-lies-bleeding," etc. And in a sickroom they are there with their fragrance and beauty to remind the sick of the love we cherish for them and to silently preach of a beauty that fades not like their own – immortal in the skies.

Their color, beauty, and fragrance command attention and are unrivaled. Christ called himself *"The Rose of Sharon and the Lily of the Valleys."* (Song 2:1). The flowers of the field were introduced into the Sermon on the Mount to illustrate a variety of truths. Consider: Solomon in all his glory was not arrayed like one of these (Matt. 6:29).

Their perfectibility. The breath of sin, the blast of winter, and the mildew of death fell upon them when they were plucked out of Paradise and scattered over the earth. That they suffered deterioration is evident from the fact that kindly culture has so greatly improved their bloom and multiplied their variety. Flowers come to us from the paradise that is past to tell us of a lost and faded beauty and to prophesy of a greater and grander beauty that shall not, like their own, so soon pass away. Music is another language of sentiment and emotion which seems to have come down to us from the paradise above – a wave of melody that has burst through the gates of heaven and overflowed its walls that our souls might be thrilled with the harmonies of the endless life and the heavenly bliss where God is praised with sinless hearts. Flowers and music tell us of the "Paradise Lost" and the "Paradise Regained" and prophesy of the beauty and harmony that shall yet prove unending when the new heavens and the new earth wherein dwelleth righteousness shall be fully established (2 Pet. 3:13).

We are also to learn from flowers the shortness of life and the corruptibility of all earthly glory. Walk through the field in its beauty and fragrance of grass and flower. The glories of spring soon pass into summer and fade away into the tints of autumn, or wither and die under the scorching heat of the sun and the fiery blast and it is all gone. David, as he tended his father's flocks, had been impressed by it and when he wrote the 103rd Psalm, he remembered it and said, the life of man is just like this; as the grass and flowers of the field, so he flourishes and so he departs. (Ps. 103:15-16; also, Is. 40:6-8 and 1 Peter 1:24).

The rose is a sign of fertility (Is. 35:1).

Flowers preach a most impressive sermon on Providence.

> What a world of thought and care
> Makes the tiny flower fair!

Destined to bloom for a day; if God is so lavish here, how much more shall not His love and care extend to His creatures who have sentient life and are capable of loving Him (Matt. 6:28-34). What a lesson is here for the man that is fearful and desponding – that is lacking in faith and hope. He ought to read this lesson every day. God will not and does not forget. If He takes care of birds and flowers, how much more will His thoughts extend to you, O ye of little faith!

But life in its unfolding here is so short – why should we grieve if we are subject to its harsh mutations? There is nothing that more keenly tries character than the sudden gain or loss of wealth. By that, the poor man's head is oft made giddy; by this, the rich man's heart is crushed and his hope and ambition fly away with his riches. But why should it be so? Life is like the flower of the grass; mutation is its order. And besides, we are tried thus sorely in order that character – the perpetual and enduring fruit of the flower – may become firm and noble and may not be unhinged by these severe blasts that sweep over it. Prosperity like adversity soon passes away and these distinctions perish in the tomb. But what if we should miss the crown of life? *"Blessed is the man that endureth temptation: for when he is tried, he shall receive the crown of life, which the Lord hath promised to them that love him."* (Jas. 1:12).

– *By the writer, and first published in the* Interior.

A Topic for Autumn

"We all do fade as a leaf" (Isa. 64:6).

In the late autumn days, the saddest of the year, Nature is preaching to us a solemn sermon from the most solemn of all texts. This lesson is whispered by every bleak wind that moans through the waning wood; it is proclaimed in melancholy murmurs by every stream that wanders through the valley, choked with the relics of former beauty and luxuriance; it is painted in brown and somber hues on every part of the landscape. The burden of every sound we hear, the moral of every sight we see is the old, old truth, which finds a ready response in every human bosom – *"We all do fade as a leaf."* (Is 64:6)

Leaves are beautiful objects – rich in color, graceful in shape, simple in structure – and they are among the most exquisite productions of Nature's loom.

Leaves fade gradually.
The whole foliage of a tree does not fade and pass away at once. Some leaves droop and wither even in spring when the rest of the foliage is in its brightest and most luxuriant beauty. Some are torn away in summer, while green and full of sap, by sudden and violent storms. The great majority of them fade and fall in autumn while a few cling to the branches all through the cold and desolation of winter and are at last pushed off by the unfolding buds of the following spring. And is it not so with every human generation? Generation after generation will come and go; tree after tree will fall and perish; forest after forest will disappear; and thus it will continue until the cycle of man's existence on earth is complete and the angel shall come and swear that Time shall be no longer and death itself shall die.

Leaves fade silently.
As He veiled His wondrous working for the Israelites at the Red Sea with the cloud of night and the complete miracle was only revealed by the dawn, so in the field of nature He reveals to us, not processes, but results. One by one the leaves become discolored and drop off but we cannot trace the insidious progress of the blight from its commencement to its consummation. The first notice we have of the change is the wild hue upon their surface. Who is to be the first to receive the message to pass hence we know not; an awful uncertainty rests upon that. The veil that hides it from our view is woven by the hand of mercy. But certain it is that some must go first. The process of decay has begun in some already.

"Leaves have their time to fall;
 And flowers to wither at the north wind's breath:

> But thou *all* seasons – all;
>   Thou hast all seasons for thine own, O Death!
> We know when moons shall wane,
>   When summer birds from far shall cross the sea,
> When autumn leaves shall tinge the golden grain:
>   But who shall teach us when to look for thee?"

Leaves fade differently.
The autumnal foliage is very varied. They all presented a uniform greenness in summer but decay brings out their individual character and shows each of them in their true colors. When death comes, the true character of each person is made apparent. *"Precious in the sight of the Lord is the death of His saints."* (Ps.116:15, precious and also beautiful. *"Let me die the death of the righteous, and let my last end be like His!"* (Num. 23:10).

Leaves fade characteristically.
The foliage that is gloomiest in its unfolding is most unsightly in its decay and the leaves that have the richest shade of green in April have the most brilliant rainbow hues in October. And so it is with man; he dies as he lives. A life of godliness ends in a saintly death and a career of worldliness and sin terminates in unrepentance and despair. The law of life is that the fruit shall be as the seed and the end as the beginning unless, indeed, the higher law of divine mercy interposes on a timely repentance. And as the fading leaf itself is characteristic, so also are the results.

Leaves fade preparedly.
No leaf falls from the tree – unless wrenched off suddenly and unexpectedly in early growth by external violence – without making due preparation for its departure. Go to the forest or the field and examine every tree or flower in this sad season of decay and you will find to your surprise and delight that there is as much of life as of death in autumn – that the elements of future resuscitation and growth are provided for amid tokens of universal decadence and corruption. As surely as

the leaf fades so we shall fade. We may imagine it distant. A thousand unforeseen foes, fatal to life, line our path on either side and we have to run the gauntlet daily between them. We began to die the moment we began to live. Our very life itself is nothing else but a succession of dying. Every day and every hour, in the changes within and without which we experience, wears away a part of it. Should we not then so count our days that we may apply our hearts to heavenly wisdom? (Ps. 90:12) – the wisdom of knowing, loving, and serving Him who alone can redeem our poor perishing life from its vanity and change it into the glory and blessedness of a, *"life hid with Christ in God."* (Col. 3:3). Apart from Him, the industry of a lifetime is but elaborate trifling, "the costly embroidering of a shroud." United to Him, our *"labor is not in vain in the Lord."* (1 Cor. 15:58) and our works shall endure and follow us (Rev. 14:13). Every leaf on the tree of humanity must fade but if we are grafted by a living faith in Him, *"whose name is the 'BRANCH'"* (Zech. 6:12), His own gracious promise becomes a living truth to us: *"I am the resurrection and the life: he that believeth in Me, though he were dead, yet shall he live; and whosoever liveth, and believeth in Me, shall never die."* (John 11:25).

> "On the tree of life eternal,
>   Man, let all thy hopes be stayed,
> Which alone forever vernal,
>   Bears a leaf which shall not fade."

– *Abridged from* Bible Teachings in Nature. (Macmillan, 1871)

Chapter 7

One Method for the Selection of Topics

I gladly avail myself at this place of some thoughtful remarks on the selection of topics and insert them here for their permanent value which were first written for the *Interior* by J. C. McClintock of Burlington, Iowa, and printed in that paper last year under the caption, "Themes from the Pews." A method like this, in the absence of uniform topics or the continuous study of the Scriptures, seems well calculated to wake up the mind of the people and lead them to take a deeper interest in the prayer-meeting and its spiritual improvement.

> "In her delightfully suggestive article, Mrs. Cooper wonders what sort of themes we preachers would talk upon if the pews gave them to us. I have wondered too and I have often feared that we missed the very subjects, sometimes, that our people most needed. We, sitting in our studies, do not always get into full sympathy with the daily life of our people. We come to them with a sermon about the philosophy of religion and they have come to us to hear how to be patient when the children are cross and submissive to Providence when business is going all wrong.
>
> "I determined to try the experiment of letting the people

select the themes that we would talk about in prayer-meeting and to see if in this way I could not get a little nearer to their everyday life and needs. So I quietly asked a number of people, representing the various classes in my church, to prepare a list of ten or fifteen subjects, such as they would like to have explained and prayed over, and hand them to me. I had a splendid response. To be sure, the topics did not differ from those I would have chosen as much as I supposed and I was glad of it. For it encouraged me to think that the pulpit and the pews did understand each other pretty well after all. But the topics were fresh; the passages of Scripture chosen to illustrate them were very well selected and I felt sure the people who made the selection would be interested in the study of their own topics. Out of the seventy or eighty handed to me by different persons, there were enough duplicates to cut down the total to about the number needed for a year. I arranged those – and it was interesting to note how they covered nearly the whole range of Christian experience, daily life, and vital doctrine – and then I had them printed in neat shape and given to everybody in the congregation.

"We had such topics as: 'The Helping Hand' (Gal. 6:1-10); 'Out into the Highways' (Luke 14:16-24); 'The Daily Walk' (Eph. 5:1-21); 'Relationship to Christ' (Matt. 12:46-50); 'Christ's Sympathy' (John 11:21-44); 'My duty to the prayer-meeting' (Heb. 10:19-29); 'Christ's Death for Sin' (Is. 53:1-12); 'The Coming of Christ' (Matt. 24:37-51); 'Planning our Business' (James 4:13-17); 'Honesty in all Things' (Prov. 20:10-23); 'How to be saved' (John 3; 14-21); 'The World for Christ' (Ps. 2:1-12).

"The result was so pleasing and profitable in every way that I have continued the plan. I am sure it has been a help to me and a great benefit to the people and the prayer-meeting.

"Why might not our churches generally unite on some such list of topics for the prayer-meeting and get the help that comes from united effort and prayer even as we have in the Sunday-School? Some time since, a correspondent proposed this in your columns. I don't know who it was, but I would like to shake his hand."

Chapter 8

The Bible and the Topics

It is our main design to present a variety of ways in which the prayer-meeting may be conducted to interest and edification. A great object will be gained if we can secure a united and continuous study of the Bible. "*Search the Scriptures, for in them ye think ye have eternal life, and they are they which testify of me.*" (John 5:39). This can doubtless be secured by selecting some book of the Bible and letting a paragraph or a section of it suggest the themes to be considered in the prayer-meeting from week to week until the book is finished.

This method is at present being followed by the Third Presbyterian Church of Chicago with Dr. A. E. Kittredge as pastor. Just now, as we learn, they are considering the Gospel of St. John. It is scarcely necessary to say that the prayer-meeting of this church is well known for its continued interest and a weekly attendance of from four to six hundred persons the year around. It would be well if, as in their case, the people were supplied with copies of the Bible at the prayer-meeting to follow the reading and its exposition or to take part in the reading whenever that is desirable. In fact, the "Bible Reading" of our day is emphasizing the importance of the people having copies of the Bible with them in all religious meetings that they may acquire readiness in turning from book to book and chapter to chapter in search of Scriptural truth, or expositions of it, as well as to acquire familiarity in the use of the Bible and become mighty in the Scriptures. In this way, the truth will pass to the heart not only through the ear but also through the eye and such assistance will prove valuable for the greater the number of senses we can employ in bringing home the truth, the deeper will be its impressions and the more lasting its influence.

This method has its peculiar advantages that recommend it in the absence of any plan that has been systematized with reference to a full knowledge of Bible doctrine in its applications to daily needs and a steady growth in grace. It has all the advantages of expository preaching. F. W. Robertson, soon after entering upon his ministry at Trinity Chapel, Brighton, announced his intention of expounding different books of the Bible on Sunday afternoons that he might secure for himself greater freedom, both in subject and in style, than the sermon afforded. In this way, he went through First and Second Samuel, Acts, Genesis, and the Epistles to the Corinthians. In Samuel, he was permitted to expound "Hebrew national life and, incidentally, the experiences of particular individuals of that nation – in all of which he discerned lessons for the English people and for the men and women who sat before him. Thus it occurred that topics of national policy, so far as bearing on individuals – questions of social life and of morals as they are connected with every-day life – arose naturally and were treated with unshrinking faithfulness." And the Epistles to the Corinthians were selected more particularly "because they afford the largest scope for the consideration of a great variety of questions in Christian reasoning which he thought it important to be rightly understood."

By this method, too, a very large portion of inspired truth will be presented at each meeting. The subjects considered will grow out of the chapters themselves and will have such progressive movement in thought, variety, and unity as the book itself possesses. In this way, truths that might otherwise be overlooked will receive proper and needful attention and the greater variety of subjects thus considered will do much to relieve the successive meetings either from being too disjointed or from being mere repetitions of the same lines of thought. "Preachers," it has been well said, "are too apt to get the truth before their congregations in one way only – whatever one they find they have the greatest facility for and that is like playing on one chord. Men get tired of the monotony. Whereas, preaching should be directed to every element of human nature that God has implanted in us – to the imaginative, to the highly spiritual, to the moral, to that phase of the intellectual that works up and toward the invisible, and to the intellectual that works down to the material and tangible."

And in addition to all this, it may give opportunity to handle certain subjects that may be particularly needed in the way of rebuke, correction, or exhortation, without giving offence or permitting it to be said that the subjects in question had been selected with particular reference to "hitting certain persons" in the church.

And finally, we will name a small number of books to be used in connection with this method and in fact with all study of the Bible which will form in itself a valuable library, or at least lay the foundation for one, in the Christian household. These are: the Bible, a Bible Text-Book, a Concordance, a Dictionary of the Bible, a Bible Commentary, a Harmony of the Gospels, a History of the Church, an Atlas of Bible Lands, a History of Doctrines, a History of the World, and Webster's Dictionary.

And as an addition to this chapter, though not intimately connected with it, we will give two illustrations to show how geography and chronology may be made the handmaids of Bible history and serve as "eyes" to the fuller understanding of Scriptural truth.

> "The physical and general geographical features of the Holy Land should be fully comprehended. Palestine proper is but a small country – not as large as Maryland and Delaware. The plan we suggest is that a few of the most prominent places, representing the various parts of the land, be selected and fixed indelibly on the memory. Their physical peculiarities, their distance and direction, say from Jerusalem, and some historical event for which they were each noted might be studied and this would help to give them distinctness. Let us take a few places as follows: Beersheba, forty-two miles southwest of Jerusalem, the old home of the patriarchs, on the borders of the desert (Gen. 21:31); Hebron, sixteen miles south of Jerusalem, there Abraham purchased the cave of Machpelah (Gen. 23:9); Samaria, thirty-eight miles north of Jerusalem,

capital of the kingdom of Israel with its wicked kings
(1 Kings 16:29-30); Capernaum, eighty-one miles north of
Jerusalem, the scene of so many of our Lord's miracles and
discourses (Luke 7:1); Dan, one hundred and nine miles
north of Jerusalem, on the northern extremity of Palestine,
where Jeroboam set up the golden calf (2 Kings 10:29);
Tyre, one hundred and six miles north of Jerusalem, the
great commercial city of antiquity (2 Sam. 5:11); Joppa,
thirty-five miles westward from Jerusalem and the port
of that city (2 Chr. 2:16); and Ramoth-Gilead, forty miles
northeast of Jerusalem, one of the cities of refuge and the
place where King Ahab was slain (1 Kings 22:3). If these
leading points are imprinted permanently on the memory
with all Scriptural incidents associated with one or the
other of them or with Jerusalem, then an important key
has been furnished for opening the sacred treasury.

"God has seen fit to convey the knowledge of His will to us
largely through history. Accordingly, in the Bible we have
the history of the way in which salvation was wrought out
for mankind, of God's providential dealings with both
good and bad men, of the condition of the race when its
Creator was discarded, and of the world both with and
without religion. We would suggest the following outline
for sacred history:

Epoch	B.C.	Name of Period	Length of Period
1. Creation..................................	4004		
2. Deluge......................................	2348	Antedeluvian Period	1656
3. Call of Abraham	1921	Noahchian Period......................	427
4. Descent into Egypt	1706	Patriarchal Period......................	215
5. Exodus	1491	Egyptian Period	215
6. Passage of the Jordan	1451	Wilderness Period......................	40
7. Establishment of the Monarchy...................................	1095	Period of the Judges..................	356
8. Division of the Monarchy......	975	Period of United Monarchy......	120
9. Capture of Jerusalem..............	587	Period of Divided Monarchy ...	388
10. Close of Old Testament History...	397	Period of Captivity....................	190
11. Birth of Christ	00	Period of the World Power	397

"These divisions of time have been made with especial reference to the history of the Bible. It will take but a very short time to memorize these ten dates and it is recommended that they be repeated hundreds of times, if necessary, so as to become perfectly indelible and familiar. The assertion is ventured that whoever does this will be astonished and delighted at the assistance it will afford in understanding the Bible history, at the order into which it will reduce the various events and at the light it will throw over the whole book."

– *Selected from Dr. Murphy*

Chapter 9

Bible Readings for the Prayer-Meeting

A praying church will be a Bible-reading church and a Bible-reading church will be a praying church. Either practice will induce the other. The revival in Bible-reading, which is so prominent a feature of the Great Awakening, shows its connection with vital godliness and the importance to be attached to it as a permanent instrumentality.

A Bible reading[1] may occasionally be introduced into the prayer-meeting to great advantage and be made to take the place of the usual remarks. This will be found, if rightly conducted, highly interesting and profitable. God honors the instrumentality of the Word, *"For the Word of God is quick and powerful, and sharper than any two-edged sword, piercing even to the dividing asunder of soul and spirit, and of the joints and marrow, and is a discerner of the thoughts and intents of the heart."* (Heb. 4:12).

To make the exercise a success, however, will require considerable study on the part of the leader; perhaps fully as much time as he gives to the preparation of a sermon, if not more. But the time thus devoted to the study of the Bible will amply reward him and repay him much more than it costs. To read and study the Word of God, to have the very words which the Holy Spirit has inspired as not merely the basis

---

1 Valuable assistance will be derived from two books lately issued: "Hints on Bible Readings," by Jno. C. Hill (Hill, 1877), and "The Hand-Book of Bible Readings," by H. B. Chamberlain (Chamberlain, 1877). Nearly all the so-called evangelists of our day give much attention to this subject and their preaching frequently is a Bible reading. And even the pastors are beginning to give much attention to the presentation of Gospel truth through the agency of what is called "Bible Reading."

of our remarks but the substance of our remarks, cannot prove other than a great blessing.

In order to prepare for a Bible reading, the leader should select some important subject relating to Biblical doctrine, Christian daily life and experience, the cultivation of piety, or the practical duties of religion. Having chosen his theme, let him next turn to his Concordance and hunt up all the Scripture texts that really bear upon his topic. Help in the selection may also be derived from Scripture textbooks: "Hitchcock's Analysis of the Bible," (Hitchcock, 1871) "Eadie's Analytical Concordance," "Locke's Common-place Book of the Holy Bible," (Locke & Dodd, 2016) "The Englishman's Hebrew and Chaldee Concordance of the Old Testament," "The Englishman's Greek Concordance of the New Testament," "Inglis' Biblical Text Cyclopedia," (Inglis, 1860) and such other books of a kindred nature as he may have in his possession. He will find it very convenient to copy on separate slips of paper each passage with the book and verse indicated from which it is taken. After he has written out all the passages having chief relevancy to his topic, he will then begin to compare Scripture with Scripture in order to classify the texts and arrange them under their more appropriate divisions. In this way, he will soon discover the harmony of Scriptures and how forcibly, as well as beautifully, they teach and illustrate his subject.

As each text is written in full and separate from the others, it can easily be changed from place to place until the appropriate place and logical order for all have been discovered and now he can take a strip of paper and pin each text in its place under its proper head and subdivision. The list of texts is now ready to be numbered 1, 2, 3, etc., in the order of sequence for the public reading. If he finds that he has several texts of similar meaning, he can select the one best adapted to illustrate his subject and make a marginal reference to the others without reading them. And between the texts, if they are pinned somewhat apart, he can jot down an outline of such remarks and illustrations as will connect the reading and give it point and application. It will not be enough to read detached portions of Scripture for in the rapid presentation of the texts alone the people might fail to catch their significance and comparative impact upon your subject.

Major Whittle has given a very serviceable caution to those who have not as yet had much experience with exercises of this sort that we do well to heed. "Be careful," he says, "not to make the reading too long. Better to divide your topic into five or six readings and bring out the Scriptures upon each head to your own satisfaction than to crowd too many heads into one reading. You will find the instruction thus given more easily apprehended and more carefully retained. The fault with most of us lay-workers, who have been uninstructed in the logical presentation of truth, is in the beginning of our work to make our readings too cumbersome. My first Bible reading on 'Faith' contained some sixty Scriptural references. Before they were all read, the audience was tired and it was a source of anxiety and difficulty for me to interest them. That same Bible reading for one meeting has now developed into *seven*, given as a course at seven successive meetings, with seeming interest and appreciation on the part of the people and pleasure to myself."

If you have adopted a list of topics for the prayer-meeting and, running through the year, you can select from this list such subjects, at suitable intervals of time, as seem best adapted for exposition by a Bible reading and then give to its preparation such study and prayer as shall serve to bring out its truths into boldness and clearness of view.

"The very best of Bible readings are gotten up by hard work," says C. Hill. "Many of them are long months in the making. In order to make these, you must search the Scriptures daily and at every turn you will find something new; note it and save it for future use. A good plan is this: have a lot of large envelopes the size of a note sheet, mark them on one corner with a topic – *e. g.,* love, assurance, etc., arrange these in alphabetical order, and whenever you get an idea, lose no time to note it on a slip and place it in its proper envelope. File away your illustrations in the same way. Scrapbooks are not well adapted to this work; too much time is lost in pasting and indexing and even then time is lost in gathering your material scattered all through the book while by the envelope system you have *all* your scraps and verses before you at a single glance. The lay evangelists Moody, Whittle, Cole, Moorehouse, and others use this method."

But as the people are to take part in this exercise, the references may be read by them in unison from their Bibles or, what will doubtless prove more efficient, by certain ones in the audience who are good readers and who, having each received a text numbered on a slip of paper prepared for this purpose, will promptly respond. And in case there should be any hesitation in the reading, it will be best for the leader to read it himself and not delay the meeting.

There are thus two methods[2] for reading and studying the Bible.

1. To read it continuously. It would be well if the Christian would read his Bible through once a year and for this purpose only ten minutes a day are necessary. More time than that is spent daily over newspapers and is not the news from heaven more valuable than the news from earth? Or it may be read by chapters at the rate of three and one-fourth a day. "I never heard of a man," says George Rodgers, "who read it right through and then said he did not believe in it. Read it all through and it will be sure to get hold of you somewhere; it will then get into the movement and become a necessity for your being; you cannot after that do without it."

2. To study it topically so as to get its collected and entire teaching on a particular subject. Such Bible reading was not possible before the entire volume was completed. During the 1500 years of its composition, the Bible was incomplete and not generally accessible but now that the canon has been closed and printing invented, the book is so multiplied that every person may possess a copy in its completeness and read and study its pages both connectedly and separately. And besides this, there are various helps to facilitate his study and guide him to a clearer understanding of the truth.

If the minister can succeed in making his church into a sort of Biblical institute for the continuous reading and the topical study of the Bible, his labors will be greatly blessed, both to them and to others as well as to himself. And if such reading of the Bible, as has just been sketched, be occasionally made the order for the prayer-meeting it can hardly be doubted that its influence and results shall be felt and seen in all areas of life and doctrine and that the Church, which is the body of Christ, shall be systematically edified and the unsaved brought to rejoice in the gracious knowledge and experience of the truth.

---

2 These methods may be particularized as follows: 1. Reading the Word:(a)Daily devotional reading,(b)Social reading,(c)Reading sacred biographies, and(d)Reading a book of the Bible continuously all the way through. 2. Studying:(a)By topics,(b)By words,(c)By references, and(d)By books.
-Presented by H. B. Chamberlain at Y. M. C. A. Conference, lately held at Baldwinsville, N. Y.

Chapter 10

Illustrations of Bible Readings

We have selected a number of Bible readings which, as examples, have peculiar relevancy to our subject – the prayer-meeting. For these selections we are mainly indebted to the two books mentioned in a footnote in the last chapter (Hill, 1877) (Chamberlain, 1877).

I. THE HOLY SPIRIT.

I. His Personality.
He is described in the Word of God as a person, and not as an influence. John 14: 16, 17, 25, 26; 15: 26; 16: 7-15. Acts 8:29; 10:19; 15:28. The words *he* and *him* should always be used, instead of the word *it*, when speaking of the Spirit.
We are baptized into His name, and He is invoked in prayer, showing that He is a person as truly as the Father and the Son. Matt. 28:19; 2 Cor. 13:14; Eph. 6:18.
Men are said to vex, to blaspheme, to resist, to grieve, to quench the Spirit, which they could not do unless He is a person. Isaiah 63:10; Matt. 12:31; Acts 7:51; Eph. 4:30; 1 Thess. 5:19.
He does those things for us that can be done only by a person, for it is He who regenerates, quickens, teaches, reproves, helps and sanctifies the believer. John 3:5; 6:63; 16:8; Rom. 8:26; 1 Cor. 6:11.
Personal acts that could not be performed by an attribute or influence

are ascribed to Him, as when He is said to knowt to reveal, to bestow power, to love, to search the deep things of God, and to distribute of His manifold gifts "to every man severally as He will." John 16:13, 14; Acts 1:8; Rom. 15:30; 1 Cor. 2:10, 11; 12 . 8-11.

It is often affirmed in the Bible that the Spirit " said " and "spake," proving conclusively that He is a person. 2 Sam. 23:2; Mark 12:36; Acts 1:16; 13:2; 21:11; 28:25; I Tim. 4:1; Heb. 3:7; Rev. 3:7; 14:13; 22:17.

The visible manifestations of the Spirit show that He is a person. Matt. 3:16; Luke 3:21, 22; John 1:32; Acts 2:3, 4.

2. His Divinity.

He is called God. 2 Sam. 23:23; Isa. 6:8, 9, compared with Acts 18:25; Jer. 31:31-34, compared with Heb. 10:15; Acts 5:3, 4.

He possesses the perfections of God ; as omnipotence, omniscience, omnipresence, holiness, eternal existence. Job 26:13; Psalm 139:7; Romans 1:4; 1 Cor. 2:10; Heb. 9:14.

He performs the works of God. Gen. 1:2; Ex. 31:3; Job 33:4; Psa. 104:30; Isa. 11:2; Rom. 8:11; 15:16; I Cor. 2:14; 2 Peter 1:21; Rev. 11; 11.

Sin against Him is sin against God. Mark 3:28, 29 ; Acts 5:9; Heb. 4:7-9; 10:29.

He exercises the sovereignty and resistless will of God. Num. 9:26; 24:2; Jud. 14:6; 1 Sam. 10:6; Neh. 9:20; Isa. 11:13; Isa. 63:10, 11, 14; Mic. 2:7; Zech. 4:6; Luke 12:11, 12; Acts 13:4; 16:6, 7; 20; 28; 1 Cor. 12:11.

We depend upon Him as upon God, Mark 13:11; John 3:5; 14:26; 16:7-14; Acts 4:31; 9:31; 10:19, 20; Rom. 8:9-16, 26; 15:13; 1 Cor. 3:16, 17; 1 John 4:13.

We are required to recognize Him as God. Matt. 28:19; Rom. 15:30; 1 Cor. 6:11: 2 Cor. 13:14; Eph. 4:30; 1 John 5:6-9; Rev. 3:22.

3. He is revealed in the Old Testament as filling men, or coming upon them, hut not as abiding with them, or dwelling in them. The Old Testament snints, while saved by the Holy Ghost through faith in the promised Messiah, were not linked to a risen man at God's right hand; but corporately and dispensationally their place was on the earth. Ex. 31:3; Num. 11:25-29; 24:2; Deut. 34:9 Judges 3:10; 6:34; 13:25; 14:6, 19; 15:14; I Sam. 10:6, 10; II:6; 16:13, 14; 2 Chron. 15:1; 20:14; 24:20; Mic. 3:8; Ex. 19:5, 6; Deut. 32:8; Isaiah 43:9, 10; Amos 3:2.

4. He is revealed in the new testament after a new Manner and for a new purpose, and hence His coming is said to depend upon the finished work of Christ. He is present now in the world to gather out a people unto the name of Jesus, to regenerate them, to abide with them forever, to dwell in them, to sanctify them, to give them their place and portion in the heavens, and to constitute them the body of which the risen Saviour on the right hand of the Majesty on high is the living Head. Acts 15:14; Matt. 3:11; John 3:5; 7:39; 14:16, 17, 26; 15:26; 16:7; Acts 19:2; Rom. 5:5; 8:9; 1 Cor. 6:19; 12:13; Eph. 2:22; 4:4; Hebrews 3:1; 10:34; 1 Peter 1:2; 1 John 4:17.

5. The Promise of the Comforter was fulfilled on the Day of our Lord's Resurrection, which was also the day of His ascension in behalf of Plis people; but the promise of the Spirit as the power of testimony and service was fulfilled on the day of Pentecost, following His visible and final ascension to the right hand of God. The same two-fold relation of Christ, first secretly to His own, and then openly in connection with them to the world at large, runs all through the Scriptures. He comes for His saints, and afterwards appears with them. Compare John 20:22 with Gen. 2:7; John 20:17 with Matt. 28:9; Acts 1:8; 2:1, 17 with Joel 2:23-32. It shows a lack of intelligence for Christians to pray for the Spirit as if He were given occasionally, or as if He had taken His departure; but it is proper to pray for the increased manifestations of His presence and power. John 14:16, 17; Acts 2:33; 4:31; 5:32; 6:5, 8; 7:55; 8:17, 29, 39; 9:31; 10:44; 11:24; 13:2, 4; 15:8; 16:6. 7; 19; 6; 20:28; 21:11; Eph. 1:17; Rev. 22:16, 17; Malachai 4:6.

6. There is a striking analogy between the relations of the spiritual to the perfect human nature of Christ, and His relations to those who are made Partakers of the divine nature. Christ as a man was born of the Spirit. Matt, 1:18-20; Luke 1:35; Heb. 10:5.
He was anointed and sealed with the Spirit. Matt. 3:16; Mark 1:10;
    Luke 3:22; John 1:32, 33; 6:27; Acts 10:38.
He was led by the Spirit. Matt. 4:1; Mark 1:12; Luke 4:1.

He acted in the power of the Spirit. Matt. 12:28; Luke 4:14-18; John 3:34; Acts I:2.

He was justified by the Spirit. Romans 1:4; 1 Timothy 3:16.

He offered Himself by the Spirit. Hebrews 9:14.

He was raised up by the Spirit. Romans 8:11; 1 Peter 3:18. See also Isaiah 11:2; Rev. 3:1. So Christians are *(a)* born of the Spirit. John 3:5, 6, 8; Titus 3:5. *(b)*They are anointed and sealed with the Spirit. 2 Cor. I:22; 5:5; Eph. 1:13; 1 John 2:27. *(c)* They are led by the Spirit. Romans 8:4, 14; 1 Cor. 6:19, 20; Gal. 5:16-18. (d) They act in the power of the Spirit. John 7:38, 39; Acts 1:8; Romans 8:26. *(e)* They are justified by the Spirit. I Cor. 6:11. *(f)* They offer themselves unto God through the Spirit. Rom. 15:16; I Cor. 12:3-13; Galatians 4:4-6; 5:25; I Peter 1:2, 22. *(g)* They are raised up by the Spirit. Romans 8:11.

7. The Offices of the Spirit in connection with the Believer.

He is the Seal. Many think of Him as the Sealer, and are in confusion about the seal ; but He Himself is the seal. 2 Cor. 1:22; Eph. 1:13.

He testifies of Christ, and never turns our eyes to the work done in us, but to the work done for us, as the ground of our consolation. John 15:26; 16:14.

He teaches in such a way that the humblest believer who is subject to His guidance is in no need of human authority. John 14:26; 1 Cor. 2:14; 1 John 2:27.

He bears witness by confirming to the heart the truth of God's Word. Romans 8:15, 16; Galatians 4:6; 1 John 5:6.

He dwells in those whom He has united to a risen Christ, and builds them together for an habitation of God. Romans 8:9; 1 Cor. 6:19; Eph. 2:22.

He is the author of revelation, and the bestower of all gifts and graces. 2 Pet. 1:21; 1 Cor. 2:10-13; 12:4-11; Gal. 5:22, 23.

He is the Comforter and Helper of the saints, and the power of their acceptable worship. John 14:16; Rom. 8:26; Eph. 6:18; Philippians 3:3; 1 John 3:24; Jude 20. Believers are urged not to grieve or quench the Spirit, while unbelievers are said to resist Him, and their sin is demonstrated by His presence on the earth. Eph. 4:30; 1 Thess. 5:19;

Acts 7:51; John 16:8. May we dwell more upon the amazing love of the Spirit. Romans 15:30.

– Dr. J. H. Brookes.

Dr. Brookes is the editor of a valuable monthly. The Truth, a publication which contains abundant illustrations of the Word and Bible readings.

How to Use the Bible With Christian Workers

Acquaint yourself with the Bible.
To use the Bible efficiently in your work, you must first be acquainted with it. Jesus says in John 5:39, "*Search* the Scriptures," implying that you must go down beneath the surface to discover the depths of the riches of the wisdom of God. In Acts 17:11, it is written, "*These were more noble than those in Thessalonica.*" Notice the stamp of nobility which God recognizes. Is it nobility of birth? Social standing? Wealth? Learning? No! Those were noble men and women "*in that they received the Word with all readiness of mind, and searched the Scriptures daily whether these things were so.*" (Acts 17:11). That is the title to nobility in God's estimation. Last winter in St. Louis, when the snow was deep, a gentleman on leaving the house one night to enter his sleigh dropped a diamond ring. It sank in the snow. No casual search for it would do. He at once placed a large box near the spot, hired the policeman to keep watch during the night, and at the early dawn made persistent search until he found it. He did this because it was something precious in his opinion. But what is a diamond compared with the riches of grace and glory which will be found in this blessed Book? Seek this acquaintance because:

(a) By it we are born again (James 1:18; 1 Peter 1:23).

(b) It makes clean (John 15:3).

(c) It builds up. Paul says to the elders at Ephesus in Acts 20:32, "*The Word . . . is able to build you up and to give you an inheritance among them which are sanctified.*" (Also, 1 Pet. 2:2.)

(d) It sanctifies and saves. Jesus says in John 17:17, "*Sanctify them through thy truth; thy Word is truth.*" (Paul says a similar thing in 2 Thess. 2:13.)

(e) It accomplishes God's will (Is. 55:10-11; Jer. 23:29).

(f) It is all powerful (2 Cor. 10:4). In Ephesians 6:17, the one weapon given for attack upon the foe is the "Sword of the Spirit, which is the Word of God."

(g) It is all-sufficient, as Jesus declares (Matt. 4:4). In 1 John 5:10-13, we are told *"He that believeth not God hath made him a liar."* Why? Simply because *"he believeth not the record that God gave of His Son."* (1 John 5:10).

All Scripture is of God (2 Tim. 3:16).
From the first word of Genesis to the last word of Revelation, *all* is inspired (2 Peter 1:19-21). *"We have also a more sure word"* (2 Pet. 1:19). More sure in one sense than the brightest flashes of glory that were ever seen upon the Mount of Transfiguration. A great many people think prophecy is a dark place. God says here, it is *"a light that shines in a dark place"* (2 Pet. 1:19 RV). They *"spake as they were moved"* not as they thought, not as they imagined, but as they were *"moved by the Holy Ghost."* (2 Pet. 1:21). Hence, Jesus, in His charge to His disciples in Matt. 10:19-20, said: *"It is not ye that speak, but the Spirit of your Father which speaketh in you."* (See also Acts 3:21; 4:25; 2 Sam. 23:2.)

Moreover Scripture is called:

(a) The oracles of God (Rom. 3:1-2).

(b) The Word of God (Mark 7:13)

(c) The Word of the Lord (Acts 8:25).

(d) The Word of Truth (2 Cor. 6:7).

(e) The Word of Eternal Life (John 6:68).

(f) The Word of Christ (Col. 3:16).

(g) The Word of Faith (Rom. 10:8-9).

I want to press this text home upon any unsaved friends. The Word is nigh to you tonight, nearer than when Paul wrote these verses. An insane woman had shut herself up in a room with a little child till both were nearly dead. When we burst into the room, we found the child lying on the bed able only to whisper, "Water, water." When her little trembling hands pressed the goblet to her lips she was scarcely able to hold it but, as it refreshed her, she seized it with a strong, nervous grasp. When your perishing, thirsty soul receives the Word of Faith, not the strength of your grasp on it but the divine power of the refreshing Word will give consolation and strength.

All Scripture is about Christ (John 5:39-47).
He does not say, "Search *part* of them." Again, read Luke 4:21; also Luke 24:25-27. Now observe, that, *"beginning at Moses and **all** the prophets He expounded concerning Himself."* (Luke 24:27). I do not wonder that their hearts burned within them (Luke 24:32). Many of the hearts of God's people have burned within them when they have found Christ in the Old Testament where they never thought of discovering Him before. In Luke 24:44-45, he says, *"All* things are written there about Me," in those three great divisions of the Old Testament. Look at what is said in Matt. 2:13-15, in the light of which read Hosea 11:1 and Acts 17:2-3. He did not reason with them out of human science, human logic, or human learning but out of the Old Testament Scriptures. Remember this when you are attacked as Christian workers by fallible science; never study the Bible in the light of science but study science in the light of the Bible. If you want to make efficient workers, build not on a philosophical basis but on the divine interpretation of God's blessed Word. Apollos was mighty in this as Acts 18:28 tells us. In the last chapter of Acts in the 23rd verse, we see Paul occupied all day with the Old Testament Scriptures. How many of us find enough in the Old Testament to occupy us all day?

All Scripture is for us (Rom. 15:4).
Believe and act as if you believed that the Word of God is for you (1 Thess. 2:13); become acquainted with its precious words and gently lead the lost into the palace of God.

The poor Empress Carlotta had escaped from the palace. Her physician knew that a rude shock would forever upset her tottering reason. Knowing her fondness for flowers, he scattered them in her pathway and she, charmed like a child, was safely led back again. If you want to become efficient workers for the Master, seek for and strew the beautiful flowers of Scripture in the paths of those who have wandered and lure them back to God.

*Cherish as Christian workers a feeling of
dependence upon the Holy Spirit.*
In Acts 1:8, Jesus impresses the importance of this dependence upon His disciples. In Acts 6:5, Stephen is *"full of... the Holy Ghost"* and in the 8th verse, we find him *"full of... power."* We also receive the spirit of adoption (Rom. 8:15; Gal. 4:6). Until we know God as our Father with child-like confidence, we cannot be efficient workers. And the child of God who is filled with His Spirit finds nothing impossible to him (2 Tim. 1:7; Matt. 17:20).

Become Efficient Workers
To become efficient workers, make use of prayer in connection with the Word (Matt. 21:21; Luke 11:9; John 14:13; 16:24). What hath God wrought in answer to prayer? (Num. 23:23; Jas. 5:17-18.)

The Value of the Soul
In your work, think of the value of the soul (Matt. 16:26; 18:10-11, 14) and of the Lord's approval (2 Cor. 5:9).
 – Dr. J. H. Brookes.

HOW TO STUDY THE BIBLE.

1. Object in study. – Find Christ (Ps. 138:2; Luke 24:27, 44; John 1:1-14; 3:11-13, 34; 5:39, 6:63; Acts 28:23; 2 Tim. 3:16).

2. Life by the Word (Deut. 8:3; Ps. 119:130; John 5:39; 6:63; Jas. 1:18-21; 1 Pet. 1:23).

3. Growth (Job 23:12; Jer. 15:16; Matt. 5:6; John 6:35; Eph. 5:26; 2 Thess. 2:13).

4. Power (Ps. 119:89; Is. 40:8; John 15:7; Rom. 10:17; Eph. 6:17; Heb. 4:12).

5. Searching in study (John 5:39; 2 Tim. 2:15).

6. Dependence on the Holy Spirit (John 15:26; 16:7-14; 1 Cor. 2:9-10, 12-13; Jas. 1:5; Jude 20).

7. With the whole mind and heart (1 Chr. 28:9; 2 Chr. 15:2; Is 26:3).

8. Seek light from any who are taught by the Spirit (1 Tim. 4:13-16; 2 Pet. 1:20-21).

9. After much study, have clear, positive views (Ps. 51:12-13; 2 Tim. 1:8-13).

Pray before reading; read and pray; search and pray; review and pray; hold fast (2 Tim. 3:14-17; 2 Tim. 4:7). Look for large results from the right study of the Word of God, for a fuller knowledge of God as Father, Son, and Holy Spirit, and for the rich and abundant fruits of the Holy Spirit in daily life (Gal. 5:22-23).

– Selected.

The Prayer of Faith

1. State of Heart. – Helplessness (Matt. 15:25). Need (Matt. 14:30). Want (Acts 16:30). Distance (Luke 18:13). Guilt (Luke 15:21). Condemnation (Ps. 51:4). Defilement (Luke 5:8).

2. Looking to the Lord. – To Jesus, the Person (Heb. 12:2). The able Savior (Heb. 7:25). The willing Savior (Matt. 8:3). The near Savior (Heb. 10:22). Jesus, our Sacrifice (1 Cor. 5:7). Jesus, our Substitute (2 Cor. 5:21). Jesus, our Sanctification (1 Cor. 1:30).

3. Confession. – Of sin (Ps. 51:3). Of specific sins (1 John 1:9). Of besetting sins (Heb. 12:1). Of past sins (Ps. 25:7). Of presumptuous sins (Ps. 15:3). Of secret sins (Ps. 19:12).

4. Supplication. – For pardon (Ps. 51:7). For purity (Ps. 51:10). For the Spirit (Eph. 3:16). For Christ's indwelling (Eph. 3:17a). For knowledge (Eph. 3:19). For saints (Eph. 6:18). For fellowmen (Rom. 10:1.

5. Intercession. – Of the Spirit (Rom. 8:26). For others (1 Tim. 2:1). For the Word (2 Thess. 3:1). For the Church

(Ps. 122:6). For ministers (Eph. 6:19). In the Spirit (Jude 20). Through Christ (1 John 2:1-2).

6. Expectation of Faith. – Longing (Ps. 61:1). Promise of help (Ps. 91:14). Promise of deliverance (Ps. 91:15). Promise of comfort (2 Cor. 1:3-5hg). Promise of rest (Matt. 11:28). Promise of gifts (Matt. 7:7). Satisfaction of all desires (Ps. 37:4).

7. Importunity. – Constancy (2 Chron. 15:2b). Delight (Ps. 37:4). Complete confidence (Ps. 37:5). Continuance (Luke 18:1; 1 Thess. 5:17). Persistence (Gen. 32:26). Repetition (2 Cor. 12:8-9). Assurance (John 15:7).

– H.M. Parsons.

What a Prayer-Meeting Should Be

1. Regular and Punctual Attendance. – Heb. 10:25.

2. Bring Others. – Num. 10:29.

3. Come Praying. – John 12:21; 15:5.

4. Continue in Prayer. – Acts 1:4, 14.

5. Avoid Criticism. – Ps. 133:1; Rom. 12:10; John 17:23.

6. Participate Promptly and Heartily in the Exercises. – Col. 3:16; 2 Cor. 1:11; Heb. 4:16.

7. Let all the Exercises be Brief. – Eccl. 5:2.

8. Keep in Mind that We Speak and Sing before God. – 2 Cor. 12:19.

9. Christian Testimony. – Ps. 40:10; 51:15; 63:3-5; 119:171-172; Isa. 43:10; Mal. 3:16-17; Matt. 10:32-33; John 12:42; Rom. 10:9-10; 1 Cor. 1:5; 2 Cor. 8:7; Heb. 3:13; Jas. 5:16.

– W. F. Crafts.

ILLUSTRATIONS OF BIBLE READINGS

THE INSPIRED PRAYERS OF THE BIBLE.

- Alphabetically arranged for private study as aids to prayer.
- Abraham, Gen. 18:23-33.
- Asa, 2 Chr. 14:11-12.
- Apostles, Acts 1:23-25.
- Agur, Prov. 30:7-9.
- The Two Blind Men, Matt. 20:30-34.
- David, 2 Sam. 7:18-29; 15:31; 24:17; 1 Chr. 29:10-19.
- Daniel, Dan. 2:19-23; 9:3-19.
- Disciples, Acts 4:24-30.
- Eliezer, Gen. 24:12-14, 27
- Ezra, Ez. 9:5-15.
- Elijah, 1 Ki. 17:20-22; 18:36-39.
- A Father, Mark 9:23-24.
- God's people, Isa. 63:15-64:12.
- Hannah, 1 Sam. 1:10-11; 2:1-10.
- Habakkuk, Hab. 1:2-4, 12-13; 3:2-19.
- Hezekiah, 2 Ki. 19:15-19; 20:1-3.
- Jacob, Gen. 32:9-12.
- Jehoshaphat, 2 Chr. 20:5-12.
- Jeremiah, Jer. 1:6; 10:6-7, 23-25; 12:1-4; 14:7-9, 19-22; 15:15-16; 16:19; 17:13-14, 17; 32:16-25.
- Job, Job 7:20-21; 10:1-22; 13:20-28; 40:3-5; 42:2-6.
- Jonah, Jonah 2:1-9; 4:2-3.
- Joshua, Josh. 7:7-9.
- The Levites, Neh. 9:1-38.

- Our Lord, Matt. 6:9-13; 11:25-27; 26:38-42; Mark 15:34; Luke 11:2-4; 23:34, 46; John 11:41-42; 12:27-28; 17:1-26.
- Moses, Ex. 3:11-13; 4:10-13; 17:4; 32:11-13, 31-32; 33:12-18; 34:9; Num. 10:35-36; 12:13; 14:13-19; 27:16-17; Deut. 3:24-25; 9:26-29; Ps. 90.
- Manoah, Judg. 13:8.
- Nehemiah, Neh. 1:4-11; 4:4-5; 5:19; 6:14; 13:14, 22, 29, 31.
- The Psalms, The entire book should be frequently read, as it is full of prayers and the devotional spirit.
- Paul, Acts 9:5-6; Eph. 3:14-21; Phil. 1:9-11; 1 Thess. 5:23; 2 Thess. 1:11-12.
- Publican, Luke 18:10-14.
- Solomon, 1 Ki. 3:5-14; 8:22-61.
- Simeon, Luke 2:28-32.
- Stephen, Acts 7:59-60.
- Penitent thief, Luke 23:42-43.

– Lewis O. Thompson.

Chapter 11

A Plan for Each Meeting

Those meetings for which both pastor and people have made suitable preparation will prove the most refreshing and successful. And just how to make the meetings successful has been one of the important subjects which the ministerial conventions held in connection with the revival labors of Mr. Moody and Major Whittle have discussed. As a result, the attention of all the churches has been aroused to the importance of the subject and the matter has been somewhat agitated by the religious press. And the answer to the whole matter is this: if we are to have successful prayer-meetings we must pray, work, and plan for them – in a word, have an intelligent plan for each meeting.

"We published last week," says the *Interior*, "some pertinent suggestions by a contributor as helps to prayer-meeting interest. We notice decided progress in the attention everywhere given to the question how to make meetings for prayer more interesting. And pastors and churches are beginning to plan for these meetings as they do for the Sunday-school service or for the Week of Prayer. People used to have an indefinite sort of idea that a prayer-meeting was self-propelling. In some quarters there has been a shrinking from studying and planning for that meeting, as if it implied some lack of reliance on the Holy Spirit. Just so, the ranters used to decry pulpit preparation, relying instead on the direct operation of the Spirit. Such blind reliance spoils the sermon.

"We are learning that, in all church work, he honors God most who is most diligent in the use of all means that tend to success.

Therefore, let every method be tried by which the vitality and power of the prayer-meeting may be secured. Let us not be afraid of having a little well-planned machinery even in a prayer-meeting. The idea that no prayer-meeting is good which is not voluntary and spontaneous in the character of its exercises should be discarded. When all hearts are full and minds alert, it will be sufficient to throw the meeting 'open,' though even then there is always the hazard that it may be spoiled by the very freedom which sometimes leads to highest success.

"But the responsibility for the prayer-meeting and its right conduct by no means rests with ministers alone. If every church member would hold his duty to be at the prayer-meeting to be as sacred as his business engagements and, being at the meeting, would refuse to be merely a sponge to absorb but would communicate according to the gift that was in him, the complaint about dry meetings would cease and the hour of prayer be, as it should be, the most delightful of all the week."

But, perhaps the chief points which a definite plan should include relate to reading of the Scriptures, prayer, remarks, singing, voluntary parts, and the length of the meeting.

Reading the Scriptures.
The portion to be read for the evening lesson should be selected with care and special reference to the illustration of the evening's subject. It is very desirable that the people should follow the reading from their own Bibles and in this way get into full sympathy with the truth to be presented as early as possible. It is often the case that a meeting does not fully wake up until it is about time to be dismissed and so it has been remarked, "If we could only begin the next meeting in the spirit and the enthusiasm with which this one closed, we should all be ready to sing, speak, and pray." "Do not slight the reading." An eloquent man is reported to have said, "If the Lord had appointed two officers in His church, the one to preach the Gospel and the other to read the Scriptures, and had given me the choice of these, I should have chosen to be a reader of the inspired Word of God." And in point of fact there is no part of any religious service that can be slighted with safety. We ought to feel that one part is as important as another and that God can bless even the minutest particular to the conversion and edification of

souls. A venerable minister testified in a clergyman's meeting that one of the most powerful impressions produced on his early life was made by Asahel Nettleton, the noted revivalist, in his reading the hymn,

> "Ashamed of Jesus! that dear Friend
> On whom my hopes of heaven depend."

The truths of that hymn went home to his heart as nothing in his sermon did. He looked back over fifty years of service to thank God that one clergyman had felt that the reading of the hymn was the great thing in the service.

Remember the Meeting is for Prayer
It should never be forgotten that these meetings are meetings for prayer and hence, undue importance should not be given to speaking nor should the remarks be allowed to monopolize the order of exercises. Prayer should be brief, pointed, and fervent. The Bible contains over a hundred prayers and these, as having been inspired by the Holy Spirit, should be our models. There are only two or three prayers in the Bible that run up to five minutes; of the rest, many of them are so brief as to have been uttered in a single breath. When Peter was sinking amid the angry waves, he did not have time for a general introduction and an eloquent speech. No! He had barely time to cry out, with intensity of purpose and need, "*Lord, save me!*" (Matt. 14:30) Had he taken more time, the waves would have swallowed him and he himself would have been past all praying. It is said that a minister over a certain charge in the East found one of his prayer-meetings characterized by delay and formalism and so to remedy this, he took out his watch and said, "Brethren, let us have *sixty* prayers in *sixty* minutes." He got them and that meeting came to be regarded as one of the most important meetings that that church had ever held.

And thus the element of time becomes very important. The interest and success of the meeting, the number that can take part, and variety in the exercises themselves will all depend upon the number of minutes that each participant consumes. In the great noonday prayer-meetings, whose interest and influence are unsurpassed, this is reckoned so important that none are allowed to occupy more than three or five minutes. What is said should come from the heart in earnest, significant words. Lengthy exhortations are not effective except in special cases. A leaf from the day's or week's experience, new light that has been shed upon some passage of God's Word, the expression of a burden or a request – some of these things that lie nearest and freshest in our hearts – we may be sure will add much to the interest and success of the prayer-meeting but beyond that, we need to have the way pointed out very clearly if we go. If we make a mistake in regard to the time, let it be on the side of brevity.

At the opening of the meeting, it would be very appropriate to have a few brief prayers with special supplications for the increased manifestations of the Spirit's presence and power. Nothing can make up for His absence. But if the Holy Spirit is present, there is no estimating the good every church may do in its weekly prayer-meetings if they but act up to their duty and their privilege.

We have already indicated in Chapter 3 how subjects of special prayer may be discovered for each meeting. As you visit your people, carry the interest of the prayer-meeting with you and be alert to discover the spiritual needs of your people that are just then most urgent, and formulate these into appropriate requests for prayer. Either before or at the time of the meeting and in connection with any written requests for prayer that may have been handed in, ask someone to pray for each particular case to the end that precious and useful lives may be spared, that the erring may be restored, that the tempted may be victorious, that the youth of the church may be led to Christ, that unconverted ones may find their Savior, that *"weak hands and . . . feeble knees"* (Is. 35:3) may be confirmed, and that grace and strength may be imparted to each and to all for the systematic growth in grace of the whole church to the glory of God. *"Pray one for another"* (Jas. 5:16).

Remarks.
Let us suppose that you have arranged a plan for the next meeting. You have given out the subject or it is already known from the printed list and you want several speakers. Very well; go and ask those you want and secure their promise to be on hand and take the part assigned them.

And that there may be considerable variety in the exercises, would it not be well to select two or three elderly persons, two or three middle-aged, and two or three young men if you require that number of speakers for each meeting? In this way, all classes will be represented and due prominence given to each. And converts especially ought to be encouraged to openly confess and acknowledge Christ. It is a critical period with them; if they now come in to be silent members, the longer they continue silent the more difficult it will be for them to speak and pray in public. At this time it is comparatively easy for them to take part for their experience is new and their hearts are full.

Singing.
This is an important part of the exercises in the successive meetings. Spiritual singing will prove half of the whole meeting in the way of interest, profit, and success. The hymns should have point and life and such natural connection with the progressive movement of the meeting that they shall fit into their place and be the genuine outgrowth of the state of feeling at that particular point in the meeting. Hence the hymns cannot, except in a general way, be selected in advance of the meeting. A meeting may be made to drag and prove tedious by the singing of long hymns lengthened by a chorus to each verse. Some have found it to be an excellent rule not to sing more than two or three verses at a time. "Let us think," says Dr. W. M. Taylor, "of what the sacrifice of praise is designed to do. It prepares the way for the descent of the Holy Spirit into the heart. *'Bring me a minstrel,'* (2 Kin. 3:15) said Elisha and while listening to the music, the Spirit of the Lord came down and he prophesied. Very frequently, through the music of the song of praise, the Spirit of God in His glory has come down and filled the living temple of the human heart. I heard the beautiful story about Augustus Toplady's conversion. He went into a barn in Ireland where he heard a primitive Methodist minister preach the Gospel. At the close, the minister gave out the hymn, 'Come, ye sinners, poor and wretched.' It seemed to him then that the whole company took up the appeal from the minister's lips and instead of one appeal there was that of hundreds. Then he gave his heart to Christ and nobly did he honor the obligation in his later life by laying on the altar of Christ the hymn that we are so fond of –

>   'Rock of Ages, cleft for me,
>   Let me hide myself in Thee.'"

Then again, singing sustains the heart in trial. Very often in this country we are in the habit of serenading our great men but oh! No songs in the ear of God are like the sounds which go up from the hearts of God's children in the night of trial. He comes forth from His throne to speak words of comfort and cheer.

Also, it braces the heart for conflict. After His last supper, Christ sang a hymn – the Lord Jesus sang and He sang with Gethsemane in view to brace Himself up for conflict with the prince of this world (Matt. 26:30, Mark 14:26). Who does not know, too, how Luther strung himself up for his Reformation work by that noble version of the forty-sixth Psalm, termed the Marseillaise of the Reformation? *"Let the word of Christ dwell in you richly in all wisdom; teaching and admonishing one another in psalms and hymns and spiritual songs, singing with grace in your hearts to the Lord"* (Col. 3:16).

Voluntary parts.
It would be wise to have a place in every meeting for voluntary remarks. It should be our object to so conduct the meetings that eventually all its parts shall become voluntary but in the meantime, so long as we cannot realize that in practice, there should be opportunity for everyone to use the privilege. There may be strangers present and these should be invited to take part. Someone may feel that he has something special to say and such should have the seasonable opportunity in which to say it. With the utmost liberty of this kind, no reasonable objection can be urged against the selection of a plan which aims to obtain continuous movement in the parts of the meeting and unity and progress in all the exercises. *"Let all things be done decently and in order."* (1 Cor. 14:40).

Length of meetings.
Uniform experience has limited the meeting to an "hour of prayer." Open and dismiss promptly. Do not wait for the people to come. Open promptly even if you are the only one there and if no one else should come, why, as Spurgeon says, "have it all to yourself; and if you are asked

how many were present, you can say, 'Four.' 'Four! how so?' 'Why, there was myself, and the Father, the Son, and the Holy Spirit and we had a rich and a real communion together.'" Also be as prompt in dismissing as in opening so that the people may know just what to expect and how to govern their engagements of friendship and business. If there is to be any variation, let it be in favor of a shorter rather than a longer session. Send the people away unwearied and they will come again.

Is it not evident that such animated interest as well-thought-out planning, working, and praying – the united effort of pastor and people – would create in behalf of the prayer-meeting would at once place and keep the church on a revival basis?

Chapter 12

Variety in Successive Meetings

Perhaps one reason why prayer-meetings are not more largely attended and enjoyed is found in their stereotype character. When you have attended one prayer-meeting of the church, you can tell what the rest will be like for you have only to multiply by fifty-two in order to get the result for a whole year. In such cases, it might be well to relieve the monotony and introduce greater variety by means of a change in the successive meetings. And with this end in view it might not be inexpedient to leave the people in doubt about the precise nature of the next meeting as to its plan that thus they may come to it in a state of expectation. Variety in this respect might do much to sustain an interest in the meetings from week to week and make them more generally attractive. Happy is he who both excites an interest and rewards it.

The continued interest in the temperance reform which, like a tidal wave, is sweeping over the land is due first to the subject and next to the method the leaders have adopted of introducing new speakers at each meeting and having, as a rule, short speeches from each. Although it is the same subject, yet the new speakers that are constantly coming forward give novelty and freshness to the theme by their varied experiences while under the power of drink and its terrible temptations and in their confessions and aspirations for a better life, they call for sympathy and help. Truth is stranger than fiction and nothing is more interesting than life in its struggles, defeats, and victories. We might learn a valuable lesson from their methods for the conduct of our prayer-meetings.

Let us then enumerate some methods of variety for the conduct of successive meetings that from these, selections may be made as circumstances require and the topics themselves will permit.

1. Conduct the meeting in the usual way and make as much as possible out of a method endeared by practice and rendered valuable by the associations of the past.

2. Let the next meeting be conducted as a Bible Reading on some absorbing theme of life and doctrine. It will be necessary for the leader to carefully collect and classify all the passages of Scripture bearing upon the chosen subject and then assign the texts to the members that they may be read in the order in which they have been numbered. The leader must secure a rapid movement for the readings and connect them by such remarks and anecdotes as will illustrate their application and teaching. At proper places, prayer and song may be introduced that thus the whole congregation may be joined together and have unity and power.

3. Variety may still further be secured by the announcement that the next meeting will be conducted on the voluntary plan. The topic should be announced, however, as nothing would be gained by leaving this an open issue. It may be stated, then, that on next week everything from first to last shall be voluntary, as "The Spirit may give utterance" and direction and in connection with this, all should be urged to come with the desire and the expectation of taking part. Urge some to come with passages of Scripture or verses from devotional hymns to read or recite at a moment when there is danger of a "long pause," and in this way the meeting will prove as profitable and interesting as any that might be more carefully arranged for.

4. After the voluntary plan has been tried, it might be well to go to the other extreme and arrange for everything so far as designating the speakers and those who are to pray are concerned. The remarks should be directed to the topic and those asked to pray should be requested to pray with special reference to the spiritual needs of the church, for the pastor, for the Sunday school, for the prayer-meeting, for the sick, for the afflicted, for the tried and tempted, and such other kindred themes as the changing and growing needs of a community would be continually suggesting. Of course, it is understood that the remarks and prayers are to be unplanned and under the guidance of the Holy Spirit. In all our

proceedings, we should seek the presence of Christ, the love of God, and the teaching and illuminating power of the Holy Spirit.

> "I need Thee every hour:
> Teach me Thy will;
> And Thy rich promises
> In me fulfill."

The prayer-meeting is not a debating society but a family meeting of the household of Christ gathered for mutual sympathy, reciprocal Christian love, and the formation of a noble character.

5. In some churches it might not be amiss to conduct a meeting occasionally in which the reading of essays and correspondence shall take the place of set remarks and exhortations. The best time for such an order would be the evening set apart to the "Monthly Concert," when a missionary topic is under consideration. It would not be difficult, perhaps, to secure correspondence from missionaries in foreign and home fields, letters from members that are traveling at home or abroad, and from former pastors and members who have gone to other churches. These would doubtless be glad to send their greetings and stir up the pure minds of the brethren to greater zeal and activity and such a method as this is entirely Scriptural for Paul concludes his first letter to the Thessalonians in these words: "*I charge you by the Lord that this epistle be read unto all the holy brethren.*" (1 Thess. 5:27). See also Col. 4:16.

And in addition to one or two letters that might be secured in this way, members of the church – and the lady members more particularly – might be asked to prepare papers on the particular topic to set forth the extent of the work in the particular field under view: the manners and customs of the people; their social, religious, and political life; helps and hindrances to the spread of the Gospel among them; their present urgent need; and other related themes. The preparation for a meeting of this kind would tend to promote the reading of history, develop a valuable literary taste, and lay the foundation for intellectual culture.

6. A change of leaders has been tried in some churches with good results. Such a method will develop the lay talent in a church, making

them feel that the prayer-meeting is their meeting and that they are responsible for its success, as well as create a confidence in their ability to conduct a good meeting. It will prevent the prayer-meeting from collapsing in case the church is without a pastor or in case the pastor is absent on duties connected with his denomination or the church at large. It will also serve to run the prayer-meeting successfully through the pastor's vacation for unless the interest is kept up continuously, the church too will take a vacation and when the pastor returns he will discover that his church has not been growing in grace but rather losing ground under the inroads of a worldly spirit.

7. Lastly, such special services as New Year's, Praise, Promise, Testimony, Thanksgiving, Experiences connected with precious texts, and Memorial-meetings may be provided for in their appropriate season.

But whatever be the method, whether the same plan is continuously followed or such variety is introduced as this chapter considers, there is no plan in itself that will guarantee success. That will depend upon spiritual conditions and the time, prayer, study, and effort which the leader shall give to the carrying out of the plan and such enthusiasm for his plans as he may be able to awaken in his people. "*Study to show thyself approved unto God, a workman that needeth not to be ashamed, rightly dividing the word of truth.*" (2 Tim. 2:15).

Chapter 13

The Importance of the Prayer Meeting

It is as important for the church in its collective capacity to sustain the prayer-meeting as it is for the individual believer to keep up his secret devotions. The Christian cannot grow in grace and in the knowledge of our Lord and Savior Jesus Christ, in spirituality and in power, without daily communion with God in prayer. This is the experience of both laymen and preachers. "Whenever a Christian backslides," says Spurgeon, "his wandering commences in his closet. I speak what I have felt. I have often gone back from God – never so as to fall finally, I know – but I have often lost that savor of His love which I once enjoyed. I have had to cry,

> 'Those peaceful hours I once enjoyed,
>   How sweet their memory still!
> But they have left an aching void,
>   The world can never fill.'

"I have gone up to God's house to preach without either fire or energy; I have read the Bible and there has been no light upon it; I have tried to have communion with God but all has been a failure. Shall I tell where that commenced? It commenced in my closet. I had ceased in a measure to pray. Here I stand and do confess my faults; I do acknowledge that whenever I depart from God it is there it doth begin. O, Christians, would you be happy? Be much in prayer. Would you be victorious? Be much in prayer.

> 'Restraining prayer, we cease to fight,
> Prayer makes the Christian's armor bright.'

"Mrs. Berry used to say, 'I would not be hired out of my closet for a thousand worlds.' Mr. Jay said, 'If the twelve apostles were living near you and you had access to them, if this interaction drew you from the closet, they would prove a real injury to your souls.' Prayer is the ship which brings home the richest freight. It is the soil which yields the most abundant harvest."

Nor can churches enjoy any great measure of success in saving souls unless they are praying churches. Praying churches will be revival churches and such will grow and prosper spiritually and temporally. Would you have a successful church? Go and get them to pray. Go and get them to cultivate the "power of the knees," not only in their closets but in their prayer-meetings. "Sirs," says Spurgeon, "I have no opinion of the churches of the present day that do not pray. I go from chapel to chapel in this metropolis and I see pretty good congregations, but I go to their prayer-meetings on a week evening and I see a dozen persons. Can God bless us? Can He pour out His Spirit upon us while such things as these exist? He could, but it would not be according to the order of His dispensations, for He says, 'When Zion travails she brings forth children.' (Is. 66:8) Go to your churches and chapels with this thought – that you want more prayer. Go home and say to your minister, 'Sir, we must have more prayer.' We must have an outpouring of real devotion or else what is to become of many of our churches? Oh! May God awaken us all and stir us up to pray for when we pray we shall be victorious. I should like to take you this morning, as Samson did the foxes, tie the firebrands of prayer to you and send you in among the shocks of corn till you burn the whole up. (Jdg. 15:4-5) I should like to make a conflagration by my words and set all the churches on fire till the whole has smoked like a sacrifice up to God's throne."

And the reason of this is evident. The Spirit is present with the believer as an unseen presence *"for He dwelleth with you and shall be in you."*

(John 14:17). The Spirit is given by measure to the believer according to the extent that the manifestation of His presence and power has been sought in prayer. To the Son, God gave not His Spirit by measure but the Spirit abode with Him in His infinite fullness (John 3:34). With men, however, He dwells to the extent of their earnest seeking and finite capacity. As the Holy Spirit is already with the believer, His presence with an assembly or a prayer-meeting must mean that each one receives a larger portion of the Spirit so that His presence is with power and demonstration. Beneath this divine outpouring, all hearts melt and they feel, with Jacob of old, "*How dreadful is this place! this is none other but the house of God, and this the gate of heaven.*" (Gen. 28:17). It was after the apostles had continued with one accord in prayer and supplication that the day of Pentecost came with open manifestations of the Spirit's presence and power. The Spirit is poured out upon the assembly either visibly as at Pentecost (Acts 2:33) or manifestly and feelingly as at a subsequent time when the disciples had prayed, "*the place was shaken where they were assembled together and they were all filled with the Holy Ghost, and they spake the Word of God with boldness.*" (Acts 4: 31).

We have all doubtless attended meetings where we felt the Spirit to be present with power and demonstration, that is, when He was poured out upon the assembly in their collective capacity and in answer to prayer (Luke 11:9-13) and was present to convict, convert, and regenerate. In the revival meetings held here last year, Major Whittle related an incident to illustrate this which he had gathered from reliable sources in Kentucky. He was told that Tom Marshall, when a student at college, was present at a revival meeting but at a certain point got up and hastily left the room for he felt, as he afterwards confessed, that he could not have held out much longer against the influence of the meeting. He was unwilling to give his heart to Christ for he seemed convinced that, if he became a Christian, it would become his duty to relinquish his cherished profession and become a preacher of the Gospel. Now where the church, through lack of prayer and consecration, is cold or lukewarm, or formal and indifferent, one is not oppressed and burdened with such convictions of duty, the Holy Spirit is not poured out upon them, and there is no increased manifestation of His presence and power. Piety will rise no higher in the church than it rises in the prayer-meeting. "I would not unite with a certain church," said a certain man, "because I know its members."

Nor can the importance of the prayer-meeting to the church and the community at large be overestimated. Heat up the prayer-meeting and the fires of secret devotion will burn more brightly. Heat up the prayer-meeting and you will heat up the pulpit. Ministers will preach with power when they have a praying church. "Oh!" said Spurgeon, "had you seen an apostolic church, what a different thing it would appear to one of our churches! As different, I had almost said, as light from darkness; as different as the shallow brook that is dried by summer is from the mighty rolling river, ever full, ever deep and clear, and ever rushing into the sea. Now, where is our prayerfulness compared with theirs? I trust that we know something of the power of prayer here but I do not think we pray as they did! They broke bread from house to house and did eat their meat with singleness of heart, giving glory to God (Acts 2:46). There was not a member of the church, as a rule, who was half-hearted; they gave their souls wholly to God and, when Ananias and Sapphira divided the price, they were smitten with death for their sin (Acts 5:1-11). Oh! if we prayed as deeply and as earnestly as they did we should have as much success. Any measure of success we may have had here has been owed entirely, under God, to your prayers and wherever I have gone, I have boasted that I have a praying people. Let other ministers have as prayerful a people; let missionaries have as many prayers from the Church; and, all things being equal, God will bless them and there will be greater prosperity than ever."

Chapter 14

How to Make Prayer-Meetings Interesting

Not the least of the services which Mr. Moody and his co-laborers have rendered to the evangelism of today is the attention they have called to the conduct of the prayer-meeting and how to make them interesting. Mr. Moody is well qualified to speak on this subject inasmuch as his experience now covers nearly twenty years of service in connection with the great noonday prayer-meetings of Chicago and his own church there as well as, since leaving Chicago, with Christian workers in England and America. His views should be attentively considered. This chapter, then, is a transcript of his talks on the prayer-meeting in answer to questions put to him in the "Ministerial Conventions," which were held in New York City in 1876 and in Boston in 1877.

The New York Convention

I think the question of prayer is one of the most important questions which can come before us. I believe more ministers fail right here than in any other place. Where one fails in a pulpit, I believe fifty fail in the prayer-meeting. I have noticed, as I have been traveling up and down the country and mingled with a great many ministers, that it is not the man that preaches the best that is most successful. You must get the people to pray.

It is so much easier to preach to an audience of people who are praying for you than to those who are criticizing you all the while. Now I find it a great help in a prayer-meeting to get the people close together; if they won't come, I would take the chair and walk down amongst them. Then another important thing is to see that the ventilation is all right. A good many meetings are held in basements and small rooms where there is no ventilation; where the windows, perhaps, won't be opened through the winter; where people get sleepy and you think it is your fault. See that it is not too hot or too cold and that the air is pure. It is a good thing to have a subject, suppose "faith" or "love," and let people know it a week before. Let the minister not always lead, for then, when he goes away, there is a collapse. If he manages right, it seems to me, he would get different leaders so that, when he goes away, there will be no falling away.

You may ask what we are going to do with those men who talk so long. Well, I would see them privately and say, "Now, try to be a little shorter." It would be a good thing, however, if the ministers would show a good example. They very often leave just fifteen minutes for the meeting and complain of Deacon Jones taking up the rest of the time. They say everything they can think of on the chapter and wonder why "the poor laymen won't take it up." Why, if they say everything they can think of on a certain chapter, there is not much chance for a poor layman especially if he doesn't know what the chapter is to be. If a man takes part in a meeting, he has a little more interest in it. There is a good deal of truth in what the old deacon said, that he always liked the meeting when he took part and he didn't care for it when he didn't take part.

A delegate observed that the Congregational churches in New England had a rule that the minister should lead the prayer-meetings for this reason – that it was found when ministers took the place of laymen in this matter, the latter took the leadership out of his hands. He asked Mr. Moody what he would do to prevent that. Mr. Moody replied that this was not his experience on the subject. Dr. Kirk, of Boston, of whose church he was a member twenty years ago, very seldom led the meeting and neither did Dr. Cuyler usually lead in his own church prayer-meeting in Brooklyn.

Q. Ought the minister to call on people to pray and speak?

A. My theory is one and my practice another. I have always advocated open prayer-meetings but very often people get up whom we know nothing about and talk too long so I have lately put the meeting in the hands of those on the platform.

Q. Is it right to call on a man to pray when he is not in the spirit of prayer?

A. He should be in the spirit of prayer but that is one of the things which makes me object to call on men to pray.

Q. What would you do with a brother who prays the same prayer over and over?

A. I should see him privately and talk to him about his own soul.

Q. Suppose you drive him away?

A. Let him go. Five will come and take his place.

Q. Is it wise to adhere to a series of topics?

A. If it is in the way, throw it overboard. Don't have a cast-iron rule.

Q. Would it be well to make the Sunday-school lesson the subject for the prayer-meeting?

A. If you have teachers' meetings, you'd better not. If you don't have teachers' meetings, I have known it to work pretty well.

Q. Shall the women take part in our church prayer-meetings?

A. It is a controversial point. Let every prayer-meeting have its own way.

Q. What about ringing the bell when a man is praying?

A. If the prayer doesn't go any further than his own head, I would have no scruple in ringing the bell.

The Boston Convention

Q. What shall we do with the awful pauses in our meetings?

A. They can be avoided, I think, if the minister is free and social and makes everyone feel at home. These pauses are just the times when that man or that lady who is not in the habit of speaking can read a verse from God's Word which they have found precious to their souls. In this way, they can gain confidence to speak. A good many people have an idea that they must follow the minister and preach a sort of sermon but a word from the Bible often carries great comfort.

Q. Would you have children in the large prayer-meetings?

A. Well, there is danger in that. One great danger which is likely to beset children is spiritual pride. A great many people in the church, unfortunately, are foolish enough, if a boy speaks for Christ in a touching way, to praise him and that makes him very proud. I should not like to have my child praised in this way. Children learn the sweetness of praise soon enough in the world. I should be a little afraid of having boys and girls encouraged to jump up in the large prayer-meetings.

Q. Do you favor boys' prayer-meetings?

A. By all means. I have found no meetings more blessed in the work of conversion. The boys and the girls should meet by themselves under the direction of some older person of experience as a leader. I have been very much interested in the meetings for little boys conducted here by Mr. Hastings.

Q. Would you announce a subject for prayer previous to the meeting?

A. I would. It has been done in our church in Chicago and it has been a great help to our prayer-meetings. We want to have these meetings a sort of family gathering where a mother who has a son out of Christ can bring him before Jesus and the whole church bear up her petition to the Lord. United prayer, in faith that God will answer our petitions, will surely bring back the blessing.

Q. Do you believe in having different ones to lead the meeting?

A. Well, that plan has been tried. Dr. Cuyler found it very successful in his church in Brooklyn. He often takes a seat among the congregation while the leader conducts the prayer-meeting. One great secret of success is to get others to work. I would rather get ten men to work than to do ten men's work myself.

Q. How ought prayer-meetings to be conducted in a church without a pastor?

A. With as much earnestness as possible. Sometimes God specially blesses a church when it is without a pastor because they trust in His grace and not in any arm of flesh.

Q. How would you break up the habit of long prayers?

A. I think ministers need find no trouble if they are honest with their people. They like real plain talk. I should speak to a man making long prayers privately, not publicly, and say to him: "Your prayers need a little more unction; they are too long for the meeting." Exhortation ought not to take the place of prayer but it is better to have an exhortation than a prayer-less prayer. That is an abomination in the sight of God and men. Some people seem to keep on praying because they don't know where to stop. Let there be always a distinct object in prayer. I have been dissatisfied at some of the men's prayer-meetings in the Tabernacle because men prayed for nothing but merely exhorted. The other night a man was telling God how great He was and how wonderfully He had made man and a godly old saint who was better acquainted with the Lord said, "Just ask Him for something."

Q. Suppose a man won't heed your advice to make prayer short?

A. I should speak to him again and again and if that did not bring about the result, I would rebuke him publicly. I would have a bell at the meeting.

Q. When do you consider a prayer to be too long?

A. Well, if the prayer-meeting is about an hour long, which I think about the proper length, it certainly can't be right for two or three men to take up the time. If a man has the cause of the Jews on his heart, let him pray for them and then stop. It is awful to open one's eyes and see that a man is teaching his own views or criticizing the opinions of other people when he seems to be praying. It chills me right through.

Q. What would you do if a man, whose piety the church distrusts, attempts to speak?

A. I would never allow him to speak. The best way is to deal fairly and squarely with people. I would rather hurt a man's feelings than to have the church injured. A man who pays fifty cents on the dollar when he could pay one hundred cents on the dollar had better keep still.

Chapter 15

Uniform Topics

If there is any advantage of having a list of topics for an entire year, would not uniformity in all the churches secure the same benefits on an enlarged scale? That system in our public schools which takes the scholar from kindergarten progressively along until he graduates in high school is wise and economical. The main fault to be found with the American scheme of education is this – that it does not extend far enough. It would be an advantage to have an international system by which all our schools should have a common basis and run parallel with each other, by successive steps, from kindergarten to the university and have such natural connection that a student would require no change in text-books and lose no rank in moving from Peoria to Chicago, or from New York to Boston. The Prussian system of education is doubtless more comprehensive than our own in this respect and it is well known that German scholarship is thorough and profound. The greater efficiency of a people, generally and systematically educated, over one less so was well illustrated in the conduct and the speedy termination of the late French-Prussian war. A gun is all the more effective for being held and controlled by a well-trained mind. The Prussian army was highly educated and prince and peasant stood side by side for the patriotic defense of their fatherland.

The writer expressed his views on this subject in an article that was published in the *Interior* a year ago which are reproduced at this place and were as follows: The fact that uniform subjects for Sunday-school study have been adopted in nearly all the Bible lands of the world shows the value that has been set upon system. Let us suppose that the Bible is so divided into chapters for daily reading and verses for the thorough and systematic study of all the facts of the Bible that the scholar is taken through the entire Bible once in seven years. Who does not see the advantage of such method in study? The feeling that all Christians around the world, on a given Sabbath, are reading and studying the same portion of Scripture is very stimulating and significant. And besides, since the time this method has been adopted, there has been a growing interest given to Bible study. It has stimulated explorations and geographical surveys in Palestine and the commentaries, maps, and helps of one kind or another called into circulation by it can scarcely be overestimated for value and importance.

Now then, would not something similar be beneficial for the prayer-meeting? If the former plan for study gives us the facts and principles of religion, why might not a series of topics be selected for each year that would be especially adapted to the needs of daily Christian life, to Christian nurture and doctrine? In many of our churches, the Sunday-school lesson has been used as the topic for the prayer-meeting. That plan has some advantages; for instruction on systematic topics is far preferable to subjects selected at random. But a little different class of topics would prove more suitable for the prayer-meeting, namely, the arrangement of Biblical truth with reference to daily life and growth in grace. Edification implies system, order, and progress. By this plan, praise and promise meetings and special occasions might be suitably provided for and all classes of Christians systematically edified (Eph. 4:12-16). This would secure unity in the services of the prayer-meeting and give opportunity for all to come with special prayer and preparation with reference to a set topic.

It may be objected that by a plan like this the special needs of a particular congregation at a particular time might be overlooked and neglected. That is true but the remedy is simple. At such a time omit the topic, make your own selection, find related texts of Scripture, and give notice in due time that the change has been made. But in the long run, nothing will be gained by making religion spasmodic. Nothing will more establish Christian life, faith, and doctrine than faithful induction into all the great Christian truths that edify the body of Christ. Is not the Bible reading and the Bible Study which form so prominent a feature of the great revival of our day; nay, is not, in part, the revival itself, under the divine blessing, a result of the increased piety, prayer and work, which the uniform lessons have been instrumental in promoting in the ranks of the laity? Would not the adoption of uniformity in suitable topics for the prayer-meeting further the same end and make Christian life more and more like the shining light in Prov. 4:18?

And in this connection the writer will add an extract from the article "On Uniform Topics for the Prayer-Meeting," which was furnished to the *Interior* by the pen of the John Locke Martin and is as follows: "The heading and its embodied idea are not original with me but I would like to add my mite of a word to help along this idea to a practical end. I have seen no suggestion of late which seems so promising of real benefit in our church work as this one of a uniform series of topics for the prayer-meeting. The very presentation of the subject should be sufficient to lead to its hearty adoption for it has everything in its favor. I know not whether the experience is general but find it to be the case with all with whom I have conversed, that one of the great hindrances toward making the prayer-meeting a success is a want of unity in the services and therefore a want of special prayer and preparation on the part of the members. To simply announce from the pulpit on Sabbath the subject for the next week-day is not enough. Very frequently some of the best attendants at the prayer-meeting are absent from the sanctuary services and so miss the announcement. But if, like the Sabbath-school lesson, there was a printed series of topics, this, out of many objections, would be avoided – everyone would know the topic. It is beyond question that the uniform system of Sabbath-school lessons has been a great help and blessing in this work. By this means, we have reaped the benefit of a system which is the key-note of all successful work and have stimulated a degree of Bible study never known before. And all of these advantages would be credited to the prayer-meeting if such a system would only be adopted by the different churches. It is simply a waste of writing to say that our prayer-meetings need all the helpful means that can be secured for have not their dullness and coldness become proverbial?"

And the following list of topics is another commentary upon the article in whose favor Mr. Martin wrote with such choice terms of admiration. And here just a word of explanation may be proper. The writer was invited by the M. B. Lowrie to unite with him "in getting up a list of subjects for the coming year for our two churches." This was accepted with the understanding that other churches should be asked to join with us. A list was then prepared by consultation, and in its present form is mainly due to the selection of the Revs. M. B. Lowrie and J. M. Waddle. A copy of it was also published in the *Interior* and other churches, if they saw their way clear, were cordially invited to unite with us in its use. So far as known to the writer, this list is now being used with profit and acceptance by the following churches: Galesburg, M. B. Lowrie, pastor; Kirkwood, E. W. Thompson; Knoxville, J. M. Waddle; Lewiston, J. F. Magill; Mt. Sterling, J. G. Lowrie; Onarga, W. D. Magner; Peoria Calvary Mission, John Weston; Peoria Grace, H. S. Beavis; and Peoria Second, Lewis O. Thompson.

TOPICS

Jan. 2	Opening of the Year	Ex. 13:10; Deut. 14:22
9	Foreign Missions, General Review	Matt. 13:38
16	Working for God Every Day	Ps. 96:2; Heb. 3:13
23	The Work of the Holy Spirit	John 16:8-15
30	Prayer for Schools	Is. 54:13; Dan. 1:17
Feb. 6	Monthly Concert, China and the Chinese in America	Ps. 2:8
13	The Helping Hand	Gal. 6:1-10
20	Sources of Christian Life and Growth	Acts 20:32; John 15:4; Deut. 8:3; 1 Pet. 2:2
27	Out into the Highways	Luke 14:16-24
Mar. 6	Monthly Concert, Mexico	Ps. 119:130
13	Why Read the Bible?	John 20:31; 2 Tim. 3:15-17
20	How to Read the Bible	Acts 17:11; Job 23:12
27	Work and Wages	Matt. 20:1-16
Apr. 3	Control of the Tongue	Jas. 1:26; 3:5-13
10	Monthly Concert, India	Dan. 7:14
17	Seed Time	Eccl. 11:6; Ps. 126:6
24	Magnify the Lord	Ps. 34
May 1	Temperance	Eph. 5:18; Ps. 94:20
8	Monthly Concert, Siam and Laos	Rom. 10:14-15

UNIFORM TOPICS

	15	The Believer's Relation to Christ .... John 15:1-8
	22	Personal Religion .... Ps. 17:4-9; 27:8; 39:1; 1 Cor. 9:27
June 5		Monthly Concert, Africa .... Ps. 68:31
	12	Christ's Love for His Church .... John 10:11; Eph. 4:11-13; 5:25-26
	19	Gospel Manna .... Ex. 16:15; Ps. 119:103; John 6:48
	26	Under the Juniper Tree .... 1 Kin. 19:4
July 3		Being God's People .... 1 Sam. 12:20-25
	10	Monthly Concert, Native American Indians..1 Cor. 9:16-23
	17	How to Keep the Sabbath .... Ex. 20:8-11
	24	My Duty to the Prayer-Meeting .... Mal. 3:16; Heb. 10:25
	31	The Promises Attending the Word . Is. 55:10; 1 Pet. 1:18-25
Aug. 7		Whom Shall I Fear? .... Ps. 27
	14	Monthly Concert, South America .... Prov. 14:34
	21	Planning for Business .... Luke 12:18; Jas. 4:13
	28	The Trials of Faith .... Gen. 22:1; Matt. 15:28
Sept.4		Monthly Concert, Japan .... John 4:9-10
	11	Advantages of Christian Society .... John 11:5; Acts 28:15; 1 Thess. 3:1
	18	Confession of Sin .... Hos. 5:15; Ps. 51:3
	25	Helps and Hindrances to Spiritual Prosperity .... Prov. 30:7-9; Lu. 12:13-21
Oct.2		The Earth Bringeth Forth Fruit .... Mark 4:28
	9	Monthly Concert, Persia .... Matt. 2:2
	16	The Danger of Neglecting the Gospel .... Heb. 2:3
	23	The Connection of Peace with Faith .... Rom. 5:1
	30	Christ's Death for Sin .... Is. 53; Rom. 5:8
Nov. 6		Monthly Concert, Europe .... Rom. 1:15
	13	The Biblical Doctrine of Conscience ..... Jer. 6:15; Acts 23:1; 1 Tim. 4:2; Heb. 9:14
	20	Visiting the Sick and Helping the Destitute .... Jas. 1:27
	27	Reasons for Thankfulness .... Eph. 5:20
Dec.4		Monthly Concert, Syria .... Acts 13:44-49
	11	Honor God with Thy Substance .... Prov. 3:9
	18	Patience under Discouragements .... Acts 27:33; Rev. 2:3-7
	25	Design of the Savior's Coming .... Matt. 1:21

Chapter 16

Steps Towards Uniformity

Let us enumerate some of the steps which have been taken by the church at large in the direction of uniform topics for the prayer-meeting.

It may be supposed that the use of the international series of Sunday-school lessons in all Christian lands and their general adaptability to the purpose for which they have been selected has given the hint to the prayer-meeting. If that has proved an advantage, why will not this also? Nor need we look upon the exposition of the topics by the religious press as tending to destroy thought, original research, and experience, not at all, but rather as illustrations of topical treatment, which, while it does not take the place of thought, may largely invigorate it and give it a hopeful, useful, and intelligent direction. And with this proof that many years of successful trial has already presented, it will be much easier for uniform topics in the prayer-meeting to step into use and favor.

Uniformity in topics for the prayer-meeting all over the world has been secured for just one week in the year – the Week of Prayer. This shows that when great results are looked for in connection with prayer, uniform action is desirable. But if this is desirable for one week, why is it not for fifty-two weeks? And will anyone say that the meetings during the Week of Prayer lack interest and profit?

The fact that some churches are in the habit of using the Sunday-school lessons as subjects for the prayer-meeting is an indication that topics with which the people may make themselves familiar are relished better than the custom which gives them no topics at all.

The seven Presbyterian churches of Detroit have united in the use of a list of topics they prepared and there is a list which was published in Burlington, IA, that has secured a very large circulation among the churches. During the year 1878, 20,000 copies of it were printed for the use of churches located in sixteen states and territories, from New Jersey to Colorado. Those who have used this list speak in the highest terms of the benefits to be derived from uniformity.[3]

But a movement on a still larger scale has already been inaugurated: the one from Chicago as a center and the other from London, towards uniformity which in the means of securing it is a great and important discovery. This plan is already solving some of the difficulties connected with uniformity. And from the sketch to be introduced, it is plain that no single person is entitled to the claim of exclusive discovery. It is evidently the prompting of that same Spirit who has access to all Christian hearts. It is generally His method, when He desires to inaugurate and carry forward a great movement, that He prepares the way for it by working upon the mind of the church at large. A perusal of the following sketch from the pen of Miss E. Dryer, will more and more convince us of this:

Bible Reading and Prayer Alliance

The object of this Alliance is to promote the united prayerful study of the Holy Scriptures. Pastors of churches, superintendents and teachers

---

[3] "For a year past a number of pastors have used the same topics in their prayer-meetings. The result has been so helpful that they are uniting in the same plan for 1878 and they ask you to join them in what has proved a delightful means of communion. The *Topics* have been furnished by several of our experienced pastors who have aimed to give a due proportion to devotion, doctrine, Christian experience, and daily life." - *Rev J. C. McClintock, Burlington, IA.*

"I have been astonished to find so many churches using *Topics* of nearly the same form. Let us have them in our Presbyterian Church, the same." – *J. M. Bishop, Lebanon, IN.*

"I am heartily interested in the scheme. We have used the list for 1877 with great profit." – *D. P. Whallon, Liberty, IN.*

"There is much good to be derived from these topical prayer-meetings. They keep the church in a chronic state of revival." – *J. M. Nourse, Athens, OH.*

"As to the 'communion prayer-meeting topics,' I am deeply interested." – *T. H. Clelland, Council Bluffs, IA.*

"I have used the prayer-meeting *Topics* during the past year, with great acceptance to my people." – *Chas. Little, Wabash, IN.*

of Sabbath-schools, and Christians everywhere are cordially invited to cooperate in this effort and to make the seven chapters of the week, or subjects taken therefrom, the frequent theme of meetings for Bible study. Any Christian may organize a class of readers and thus many unsaved persons may be brought to the teaching of the Word of God.

The Committee who recommend this Alliance is composed of representatives chosen by their respective denominations and societies in the city of Chicago, to promote this work.

T. W. Harvey, Pres. Y. M. C. A., Chairman.
Bishop C. E. Cheney, Reformed Episcopal.
Dr. D. B. Cheney, Baptist.
Dr. J. Monro Gibson, Presbyterian.
Dr. E. P. Goodwin, Congregationalist.
Dr. Edward Sullivan, Episcopal.
Dr. John Z. Torgerson, Lutheran.
Dr. W. C. Willing, Presiding Elder, M. E. C.
Mrs. W. H. Goodrich, Bible Work, Cor. Sec. and Treas.
Miss E. Dryer, Bible Work, Rec. Sec.

The Bible Reading and Prayer Alliance had its beginning on January 1st, 1877, in a small morning prayer-meeting in Chicago. There was then no purpose of extending it beyond the circle of a few Christian friends. But, in God's providence, so rapidly did the united interest spread that a Scripture Calendar was prepared and very soon the first five thousand had found their way, *with care,* into churches, Sunday-schools, hospitals, boarding-houses and families, not only in the city but in different parts of the state and in distant states.

The effort received its first marked impulse in a conference of Christian ladies of different denominations who met weekly for Bible study and prayer (most of whom were engaged in the active Christian work of cottage prayer-meetings and house to house visitation) which attended and followed the Moody meetings of that winter.

These Christian workers were bound together, under the name of the "Bible Work Association," by the following agreement:

We, the undersigned, purpose

To read the Bible together daily, praying the Holy Spirit to guide us into all truth, according to our Lord's promise: John 16:13.

To pray daily for each other, that we may grow in grace and a knowledge of our Lord Jesus Christ: 2 Pet. 3:18.

To meet together weekly and monthly for prayer and conference and study of the Scriptures that we may thereby be better prepared to present to the lost, salvation in Jesus Christ and to lead His church to seek the things that are above where He sitteth on the right hand of God: Col. 3:1.

By personal conversations, prayer-meetings, Scripture readings, and other Christian efforts, to present Christ as the Savior of the lost and to present help to all who are weary and heavy laden: Matt. 11:28.

In a few months, it was evident that the Lord was extending the work beyond the control of any such organization of active membership as was at first contemplated and yet not a line had appeared in print concerning it.

In June, the secretary learned through a newspaper item that in January 1876, a similar union was formed in London under the leadership of the Thomas Richardson which numbered about 18,000 members the first year and which had extended, through missionaries, to Arabia, China, Persia, and India.

It then became more than ever apparent that our Lord was executing a loving purpose of uniting His Church in prayer and Bible study in a new and great degree, and increased and systematic efforts were made to establish the wide-spread work which had grown from such small beginnings.

The present Committee, representatives of evangelical denominations and societies in Chicago, convened in October 1877 and, under the new name, organized to promote the objects of this Alliance. It was thought best to spend six months in the New Testament and six months in the Old Testament: beginning in January with Matthew and reading the first two gospels and the epistles of Paul and in June to begin Genesis, reading historic parts of the Old Testament during the remainder of the year.

From these Daily Readings, the committee has selected fifty-two topics which, following the practice instituted at the beginning, may be conveniently used in weekly meetings and which present the advantage of united study and preparation on the part of those who use them.

A similar course has, during the last year in some parts of our country, been followed with good results in church prayer-meetings, cottage meetings, and meetings organized for Bible study.

We hope that in churches, Sabbath-schools, and Christian communities, Christians who are interested to forward this Union of Bible study and prayer will send us their names at once. We shall issue cards of membership to such and to all others who, for the year, desire them.

To induce others to read the Bible systematically is one of the *easiest* and *most fruitful* sources of Christian effort.

Old and young, sick and well, may find successful work in this line. One feeble Christian, in a community where there is no church may, through faith and prayerful effort, form a society in which the Word of God shall grow until the sower and reapers shall rejoice together in heaven amid the gathered harvest (Deut. 8:3; Matt. 13:3-9; John 15:3; Acts 6:7; 17:11; Col. 1:5-6).

God has promised *to bless His own Word* (Is. 55:10-11; Matt. 24:35).

And in order to secure uniformity in the study of God's Word, the committee also prepared a Calendar for Daily Scripture Readings and, in connection therewith, a list of topics for the weekly prayer-meetings.

The adoption of some such plan as this would prove a powerful supplement to the daily cultivation of piety as set forth in our fourth chapter. And it has these conspicuous merits: it secures uniformity, the topics grow out of the daily readings, and the daily readings prepare for the topics and help to illustrate them. All in all, it is a most admirable combination and possesses such features as ought to recommend its adoption to all who are earnestly praying for salvation in Israel and the more general establishment of our Redeemer's kingdom. Fly, O thou angel having in charge to preach the everlasting Gospel unto all them that dwell on the earth, and to every nation, and kindred, and tongue, and people, and say to them all, Fear God, love, honor and obey Him (Rev. 14:6-7).

But whether we shall have uniform topics or not, either on a limited or a general scale, let us have interesting prayer-meetings. Let us set to work with such earnestness and let us adopt such methods as, under the divine blessing, shall secure them.

Chapter 17

Helps for Speaking in Public

Those who attempt to speak in public for the first time need to be told that the agitation of mind which often accompanies the effort is not peculiar to themselves but is an experience common to all, or nearly so, and is not to be taken as a sign that they will never be able to speak with freedom and delight.

There may be some who are natural orators who seem to be born such and to such, like the poet of whom Horace writes, and to such nothing need be said. They take to speaking as naturally as ducks to water. The perfect orator is one who knows everything and is always prepared, knows just what to say, how to say it, and when to say it. His will power is so imperial that nothing can daunt or subdue it, against whom the storms of opposition beat in vain. His sensibilities are so tender that they are responsive to every emotion and so deep as to impress every hearer. He is like the lake on whose surface every breeze makes an impression and from whose depths the storms stir up the waves that sweep the sky and carry everything along with them. The trembling heart and the responsive eye give proper tones to expression and suitable look and gesture to every action.

The majority of mankind are less gifted and need to study and premeditate in order to know what to say. They need to practice in order to learn how best to say it and by frequent trial on the waves of impromptu speech, acquire the secret of speaking with force, vigor, precision, and persuasion. If there is any comfort in that, there are many examples of those who at the outset have made miserable failures. The case of Sheridan is well known. His "maiden speech" in the House of Commons was a failure that nearly drove him wild, but not to despair, for he immediately vowed "That it was in him and should come out." He persevered and became one of the most brilliant orators in English history. The life of Disraeli, the present Earl Beaconsfield, furnishes an example exactly similar to that of Sheridan's.

It is related of David Livingstone, the African explorer, that the first time he tried to preach for a minister who was ill, he could get out nothing beyond the text and after repeated trials he walked down the steps of the pulpit, took up his hat, and went away leaving sermon and service unfinished.

It is said that when the poet Longfellow visited London, he accepted the compliment of a breakfast on the express condition that there should be no public speaking. But some clever man purposely laid a trap for him, got up, and toasted him in some very complimentary remarks. These called for a response from the poet. In his embarrassment, he arose and attempted a speech but could get out nothing but something like this: "Gentlemen, I thank you."

When Dr. Windship, the Yankee Hercules, first appeared with a lecture before a Boston audience to tell how he had acquired his immense strength, he was so overcome by the sight of his audience as to faint in their presence but immediately upon recovering and learning the cause of his discomfiture, he said: "What! a man that can lift two thousand pounds afraid of an audience, impossible! Let me go before them again, I will and must tell them what I have to say" – and tell them he did.

John Stuart Mill frequently halted in his speeches, and yet was a very forcible and clear speaker. But I need not multiply instances to prove that men of profound thought and great ability have experienced great difficulty in acquiring the habit of impromptu speech.

The majority of those who have succeeded as public speakers have taken considerable pains to perfect themselves in oratory. It is related of Joseph Cook, by those who know him intimately, that even when he was a mere boy, he liked nothing better than to go into the open air and speak spontaneously on some random subject and all through his course of study at the academy and college, he gave particular attention to the practice of oratory.

It is said that Henry Clay, in early life, practiced in a barn where the astonished cattle were his audience. During many years, Newman Hall spent fifteen minutes each day in the practice of impromptu speech and took his subject from whatever page of his Bible to which he opened at random. The example of Demosthenes is so often alluded to as to be threadbare but yet no example is more pertinent, for he has stood in all ages as the acknowledged master of eloquence. It was by the utmost diligence he became such. You will remember how he spoke before the waves of the surging sea that the roar of a multitude might cease to be terrifying; you will remember how he overcame shortness of breath and an impediment in speech by running up hills and articulating words with pebbles in his mouth. Very pertinently has Cicero condensed an all-important rule for success into a threefold practice for when asked," What was the first requisite for oratory?" he replied, "Action."

"What is the second?"

"Action."

"What is the third?"

"Action."

But, as a general thing, those who take part in a prayer-meeting do not contemplate the acquisition of oratory to the extent in which the masters of eloquence have acquired it. They will be content if they can speak upon a subject with comfort to themselves and edification to others and offer prayer in such phrases as shall indicate their sincerity and not show that they have more zeal than knowledge. Let us enumerate some principles that may serve as helps in this direction.

An excellent help will be to meditate frequently upon your subject and even to pray over it. This will prove a suitable soil for the reception of your subject out of which shall grow the tree of thought with its fruit of effective expression for public speech.

Then, again, talk about your subject with others. In efforts to explain it, suitable words will come and with them a fuller understanding of the subject and oft times new ideas from those with whom you converse. Such exercise, like the whirl of the sling before the stone is cast or the bend of the bow before the arrow flies, will give momentum to your thought and send it to the brow of conviction.

And as you know what the subject will be on which you desire to speak, gather up illustrations from your own experience, from your walks in daily life, from your work and business, and from the company you keep. Keep your eyes and ears open and you will find "tongues in trees, books in the running brooks, sermons in stones, and good in everything." Truly the attentive listener will hear the grass grow and at every step in life find illustrations that shall prove feathers to guide the arrow of discourse in its flight and barbs to make it stick.

It will be wise, also, to read on your subject. If you digest and assimilate what you read, this will enrich your own thoughts and make what you shall say all the more valuable. It will also help you to have more accurate expression in speech if you write on your subject. "Reading maketh a full man, conference a ready man, and writing an exact man." But, if you write, it should not be with a view to committing it to memory for this will always keep you in bondage and prevent you from acquiring the larger liberty of impromptu speech. It was the saying of Pulteney, the first Earl of Bath, that there are "few orators who commence with set speeches," and in practicing on this rule he became one of the leading speakers in Parliament.

And these various parts in preparation will prove so many steps by which your subject shall work itself down into your own heart. The home of eloquence is the heart, for oratory, like music, poetry, and painting, springs from the heart. "The greatest thoughts do not spring from the understanding but enter into it from the heart of man; the heart is the bud of the head." To be devoid of feeling is to be devoid of eloquence. When we feel deeply, we think clearly and talk freely. "If you wish me to weep," says Horace, "you must first weep yourself."

"My heart was hot within me," says the Psalmist, "while I was musing the fire burned: then spake I with my tongue" (Ps. 39:3). So likewise Jeremiah: "But his word was in mine heart as a burning fire shut up in my bones, and I was weary with forbearing and I could not stay." (Jer. 20:9). Without heart in them, thoughts may be ever so clear but they will be lacking in that warmth which eloquence produces; they may dazzle but they will come as cold as a beam of light from an iceberg.

Another excellent rule for speech in the prayer-meeting is this: be brief. This was Luther's suggestive adage: "Get up boldly; open your mouth widely; be done quickly." If you set out to speak half an hour, you might find it very difficult to fill the time but if you get up with something to say that you must say, born of such preparation as has been indicated, when you have poured out your thought, stop. When you are through, have done. There is many a man that does not know when to stop but flies like a wounded bird from bush to bush till he drops by sheer exhaustion. John Bright, "the great commoner," when interviewed said, "The only part of my speech that I prepare in set words is the conclusion. I always know how and when I am going to stop." Be content to say a few things well, rather than many poorly. When it shall become the rule to speak as briefly as possible, we shall find that we have more to say than we thought we had, that it is easier to speak than we thought it was, and that what we say goes straighter to the mark than we thought it would.

But whatever be the result of your attempts to speak in public, do not be discouraged. Do not be prevented from having your say, though your mind be agitated, and the trepidation promises to stick by you through life. The agitation of your mind may arise from physical peculiarities. It is difficult to control one's temperament and compel shaking knees to stand still. But this will prove no serious hindrance to your success as a speaker if you will only accept it as a fact and press forward with invincible resolution. Cicero has said of himself that "he grew pale at the beginning of a speech and felt a tremor in every part of his frame." And of his first attempt he said, "I was so intimidated that (I speak it with the highest sense of gratitude) Quintus Maximus adjourned the Court, when he perceived me thus oppressed and disabled with concern." Nor are some of the bravest and boldest ministers, who have seen years of service, strangers to this certain trouble. "I am now an old man," said Luther, "and have been a long while occupied in preaching, but I never ascend the pulpit without a tremor."[4]

---

[4] Timidity is a more general characteristic of public speakers than is generally supposed. From the references made to this subject in "The Life and Letters of Lord Macauley," (Trevelyan, 1876) we would infer that he himself, although a most brilliant speaker, was not free from this trouble. In writing to Mr. Ellis, he says: "Why did not Price speak? If he was afraid, it was not without reason for a more terrible audience – the House of Commons – there is not in the world. Tierney used to say that he never rose in the House without feeling his

It is a twice-told tale. There are none who cannot become effective speakers if they set out with a determination to conquer, even if it takes all summer. "The gods sell us everything for labor," says an old Greek proverb. Intelligent and continuous practice will achieve success and produce a certain measure of freedom. Perhaps the example of Mr. Moody is as good as any that can be found in the way of encouragement. One could hardly have more obstacles in the way than he had. Mr. William Reynolds related the following interesting reminiscence at a convention held in Canada three or four years ago: "The first meeting I ever saw him at, was in a little old shanty (in Chicago) that had been abandoned by a saloon-keeper. Mr. Moody had gotten the place to hold a meeting in at night. I went there a little late and the first thing I saw was a man standing up, with a few tallow candles around him, holding a negro boy and trying to read to him the story of the Prodigal Son and a great many of the words he could not make out, and had to skip. I thought, if the Lord can ever use such an instrument as that for His honor and glory, it will astonish me. After that meeting was over Mr. Moody said to me, 'Reynolds, I have got only one talent: I have no education but I love the Lord Jesus Christ and I want to do something for Him and I want you to pray for me.' I have never ceased from that day to this, morning and night, to pray for that devoted Christian soldier. I have watched him since then, have had counsel with him, and know him thoroughly and for consistent walk and conversation I have never met a man to equal him. It astounds me when I look back and see what Mr. Moody was thirteen years ago and then what he is under God today – shaking Scotland to its very core, and reaching now over

---

knees tremble under him and I am sure that no man who has not some of that feeling will ever succeed there." This anxiety then argues better for our success than could have been supposed. And, again, in a letter to his sister, he writes: "We – at a dinner party at Lord Althorp's - talked about timidity in speaking. Lord Althorp said that he had only just got over his apprehension. 'I was as much afraid,' he said, 'last year as when first I came into Parliament. But now I am forced to speak so often that I am quite hardened. Last Thursday I was up forty times.' I was much surprised at this in Lord Althorp, as he is certainly one of the most modest men in existence. But I was surprised to hear Stanley say that he never arose without great uneasiness. 'My throat and lips,' he said, 'when I am going to speak, are as dry as those of a man who is going to be hanged.' Nothing can be more composed and cool than Stanley's manner. His fault is on that side. A little hesitation at the beginning of a speech is graceful and many eminent speakers have practiced it in order to give the appearance of unpremeditated reply to prepared speeches. Stanley speaks like a man who never knew what fear, or even modesty, was. Tierney, it is remarkable, who was the most ready and fluent debater almost ever known, made a confession similar to Stanley's. He never spoke, he said, 'without feeling his knees knock together when he rose.'"

to Ireland. The last time I heard from him, his injunction was, 'Pray for me every day; pray now that God will keep me humble.'"

Public speaking at the outset may prove like the efforts of a boy learning to skate. It is attended with many a fall and bruise but presently that which in the beginning was so slow and dangerous, becomes safe and delightful. How well I remember what a pleasure skating became after I had learned how to skate. With what bounding joy I rushed forward the moment I caught sight of the river, with what eager haste I buckled on my skates, and with what ecstasy of delight I flew away over the frozen field as it lay beneath my feet like a mirror glittering in the sun – it was a thing of beauty and a joy forever."

Is not the experience of Mr. Moody something like this? It cannot now be otherwise than the greatest joy for him to speak with such freedom, power, and perfect command of himself and his audience. Be content to fail a number of times, if that is necessary, but "don't give up the ship." Be encouraged by his noble example and say that "I dare not wait upon I would":

> I would, but cannot sing,
> I would, but cannot pray,
> I would, but cannot speak.

With reasonable effort and perseverance, we shall conquer a reasonable and enjoyable fluency in speech and prayer – not for its own sake but that, as living witnesses to the power of truth, God may take our words and make them suitable instruments of persuasion to the edification of the church, the conversion of sinners, and the advancement of His Kingdom.

Chapter 18

Aids to Secret, Social, and Public Prayer

Prayer is the loving communion of the soul with God, the conversation of a child with his Father in heaven. In prayer, we consciously draw near to God in faith to praise and magnify His great and holy name, to thank Him for life's unnumbered mercies, to make confession of our sins, to ask for pardon, to entreat Him for new supplies of grace for the conduct of each day, to obtain His assistance in the many needs and emergencies of life, to seek the guidance of the Spirit in the exercises of worship, and to offer all our desires in the name of our Advocate and for the sake of our great Redeemer.

Prayer is likewise daily to be offered up to God as the occasion requires, whether it be in secret, in the family, or in the circle for public prayer. Each day brings its peculiar circumstances and so each day requires new and peculiar grace to meet them. We can no more pray for the spiritual needs of our lives a year, month, or week in advance by a single prayer, than we can eat at a single meal sufficient to suffice for the physical needs of a year, month, or week. Our physical needs are such that we should consider it a peculiar hardship if we could not minister to them at least three times a day. Can the spiritual man within us be more easily nourished and not need ministering unto but once a month or year?

"To prayer, to prayer! for the morning breaks,
    And earth in her Maker's smile awakes;
His light is on all below and above,
    The light of gladness and life and love.
O, then, on the breath of this early air,
    Send upward the incense of grateful prayer!

"To prayer! for the glorious sun is gone,
    And the gathering darkness of night comes on.
Like a curtain from God's kind hand it flows,
    To shade the couch where His children repose.
Then kneel, while the watching stars are bright,
    And give your last thoughts to the Guardian of night."

A full and comprehensive prayer will include:

First, adoring the glory and perfections of God as they are made known to us in the works of creation, in the conduct of Providence, and in the clear and full revelation He hath made of Himself in His written Word.

Second, giving thanks to Him for all His mercies of every kind, general and particular, spiritual and temporal, common and special; above all, for Christ Jesus, His unspeakable gift, and the hope of eternal life through Him.

Third, making humble confession of sin, both original and actual, acknowledging and endeavoring to impress the mind of every worshipper with a deep sense of the evil of all sin as being a departure from the living God and also taking a particular and moving view of the various fruits which proceed from this root of bitterness: sins against God, our neighbor, and ourselves; sins in thought, in word, and in deeds; sins secret and presumptuous; sins accidental and habitual. Also, the aggravations of sin, arising from knowledge, or the means of it; from distinguishing mercies; from valuable privileges; from breach of vows, etc.

Fourth, making earnest supplication for the pardon of sin and peace with God, through the blood of the Atonement, with all its important and happy fruits; for the Spirit of sanctification and abundant supplies of the grace that is necessary for the discharge of our duty; for support and comfort under all the trials to which we, being sinful and mortal, are liable; and for all temporal mercies that may be necessary in our passage through this valley of tears, always remembering to view them as flowing in the channel of covenant love and intended to be subservient to the preservation and progress of the spiritual life.

Fifth, pleading from every principle warranted in Scripture, from our own necessity, the all-sufficiency of God, the merit and intercession of our Savior, and the glory of God in the comfort and happiness of His people.

Sixth, intercession for others including the whole world of mankind; the kingdom of Christ or His church universal; the church or churches with which we are more particularly connected; the interest of human society in general and in that community to which we immediately belong; all that are invested with civil authority; the ministers of the everlasting Gospel; and the rising generation along with whatever else more particular may seem necessary or suitable to the interest of the people with whom we worship or of the family with which we live and of which we are a part.

But it will be doubted whether any single prayer should include all the enumerated particulars; at least, there is no prayer to be found in the Bible that is as full and comprehensive as the outline above would indicate. The Bible gives us, as to the length of any prayer, what I would call three classes of models: first, those that are very brief, hardly more than the heaving of a sigh or the utterance of a single breath, like the publican's prayer (Luke 18:13); second, those of medium length, like the Lord's prayer (Matt. 6:9-13) or the prayers of Elijah (1 Kin. 18:36-37); and third, those of greater length, like the prayer of temple dedication (2 Chr. 6:14-42), the Levite's prayer (2 Chr. 30:27), or the high-priestly prayer of our Lord and Savior (John 17).

We should be encouraged in the frequent practice of prayer by the commands of the Bible to pray and the promises of God to hear and answer prayer. This makes prayer something more than a subjective exercise, an introspection, or practice in oratory. *"Wait on the Lord: be of good courage, and He shall strengthen thine heart: wait, I say, on the Lord."* (Ps. 27:14). *"As for me, I will call upon God: and the Lord shall save me. Evening, and morning, and at noon, will I pray, and cry aloud: and He shall hear my voice."* (Ps. 55:16-17). *"The sacrifice of the wicked is an abomination to the Lord: but the prayer of the upright is His delight."* (Prov. 15:8). *"The Lord is far from the wicked: but He heareth the prayer of the righteous."* (Prov. 15:29). *"He giveth power to the faint; and to them that have no might He increaseth strength. Even the youths shall faint and be weary, and the young men shall utterly fall: but they that wait upon the Lord shall renew their strength; they shall mount up with wings as eagles; they shall run and not be weary; and they shall walk and not faint."* (Is. 40:29-31). *"Ask and it shall be given you; seek and ye shall find; knock and it shall be opened unto you"* (Matt. 7:7). *"And He spake a parable unto them to this end, that men ought always to pray, and not to faint"* (Luke 18:1). *"Be ye therefore sober and watch unto prayer"* (1 Pet. 4:7).

Prayer brings the soul into spiritual communion with God and there is as direct a line of communication from earth to heaven by its instrumentality as there is between the cities of the land by means of the electric wire and current. How curious are the revelations of the telephone. You desire to talk with a man many miles distant, you step to the apparatus, you touch a key, it rings a bell in his office, and in response to the signal he takes his place by the receiving mechanism and now he hears you as plainly as if you were standing by his side or in the next room. With such an illustration of capabilities to be used in the realm of nature, is it difficult to imagine how prayer may ring a bell in heaven? Is it difficult to imagine how prayer may avail itself of those subtler and more powerful resources and currents that belong to mind and spirit in the realms of grace and glory and have its petitions not merely transmitted but even the very tones of the voice rendered audible at the throne of grace? Aye, verily, there are more things in heaven and earth than are dreamed of in our philosophy.

> "More things are wrought by prayer than this world dreams of;
> For what are men better than sheep and goats
> That nourish a blind life within the brain,
> If, knowing God, they lift not hands of prayer,
> Both for themselves and those who call them friends?
> For so the whole world round is every way
> Bound by gold chains around the throne of God."

It will be an aid to us in prayer if we get a clear understanding of the topics of prayer and for this knowledge we must consult the Bible. And I, for one, believe that prayer in our day avails for just the same things that it availed in the days of the apostles, prophets, and worthies of the olden days – that its measure is faith, that its rule is the will of God, that its inspiration is from the Holy Spirit, and that its object is the glory of God and the spiritual improvement of self and fellow-man.

In the Bible we learn that prayer has availed for:

- rain (Jas. 5:17-18, 1 Kin. 17:1, 19:41-46),

- restoration from sickness and death (2 Kin. 4:32-35),

- "good speed" in fulfilling the terms of a commission (Gen. 24:12),

- deliverance from a brother's hostility (Gen. 32:9-11),

- God's assistance in leading a nation out of bondage (Ex. 2:23, 3:7-10),

- influencing the minds of others (Esth. 4:16),

- healing from leprosy (Luke 5:12-13),

- guidance and rescue in critical junctures (2 Chr. 20:1-30),

- favor in old age (Is. 38:5),

- removal of affliction (Deut. 26:7-8),

- a blessing upon the household (Deut. 3:1,11, 2 Sam. 6-11),

- nearness to God (Jas. 4:8),

- the verification of divine promises and covenant mercies (1 Kin. 8:22-56),

- Divine interventions in behalf of true religion and the glory of God (Dan. 2:17-19),

- assistance and favor in rebuilding the temple of God and the homes of a desolate city (Ez. 1:1-2, Neh. 1:4-11),

- the forgiveness of sin and the pardon of iniquity (Ps. 25:11),

- removal of vanity and lies far from the heart (Prov. 30:7-8),
- peace and prosperity (1 Chr. 4:10),
- reformation after national apostasy (2 Chr. 7:14, Jon. 3:8-10),
- rescue from imminent perils (Matt. 14:30),
- revival of grace (Ps. 84:8, 11),
- deliverance from evil (Matt. 6:13),
- departure in peace from this life after fulfillment of a promise (Luke 2:29),
- mercy in case of blindness (Matt. 9:27-30),
- help to a sick child (1 Kin. 17:21-23),
- remembrance in the kingdom of glory (Luke 23:42),
- direction in the issue of the lot (Acts 1:24-26),
- boldness to speak and preach the Word (Acts 4:29),
- opening doors of usefulness (Acts 10:9, 16:26),
- the right improvement of opportunities (2 Sam. 7:27),
- removal of sin from those not knowing what they do (Luke 23:34),
- knowledge of what one must do in order to please God (Num. 22:34),
- the fullness of the Spirit in the heart (Ezek. 36:26; 1 Thess. 5:23),
- wisdom to supply lack and need (Jas. 1:5),
- wisdom to remove difficulties and conquer temptations (Matt. 26:41),
- growth in knowledge of the truth (Col. 1:9),
- richer abundance in spiritual attainments (2 Thess. 1:11-12),
- the varied graces of faith, hope, and love (Phil. 1:9)

- the continuous acquisition of every virtue to adorn character, ripen manhood, dignify womanhood, and make life both here and hereafter grow up in all things after the pattern of Christ, till the fruit shall be full sanctification; in a word, for help in the realm of nature, for guidance and protection in the realm of providence, for spiritual growth in the realm of grace, and for full fruition in the realm of glory (John 17:17, 20).

A very wealthy man cannot be richer than the Christian who lives up to the full privileges of his adoption and fully believes that he is an heir of God and joint-heir with Christ to an inheritance that is *"incorruptible and undefiled and that fadeth not away"* (1 Pet. 1: 4). *"All things are yours"* (1 Cor. 3:21b). *"According to your faith be it unto you."* (Matt. 9:29b). *"For verily I say unto you, that whosoever shall say unto this mountain, Be thou removed, and be thou cast into the sea; and shall not doubt in his heart, but shall believe that those things which he saith shall come to pass; he shall have whatsoever he saith. Therefore I say unto you, what things soever ye desire when ye pray, believe that ye receive them, and ye shall have them."* (Mark 11:23-24).

And in these and kindred topics of prayer we are to ask for others as well as for ourselves. There are those whom we can help in no other way, whom we can meet in no other way, whom we can meet and help in prayer. The mother's prayer for her absent child reaches far over the ocean and on distant seas puts peace into his heart and wisdom into his mind for the pressing needs he faces.

> "There is a scene where spirits blend,
>   Where friend holds fellowship with friend;
> Though sundered far, by faith they meet,
>   Around one common mercy-seat."

Nor are we to regard answers to prayer as forming any violation of the laws of nature for the realm of nature works into that of grace and is subordinate to it. These and whatever other realms there may be combine to form one kingdom, a grand universe, a beautiful cosmos under one code of laws and uniform administration and subservience. The lever which regulates each realm reaches to the throne of God and the Hand of omnipotence and omniscience controls them. The Christian who prays in faith enters into the use of one of the great forces which God has designed, with especial reference to lifting man out of a lower realm and preparing him for entrance into a higher one.

But even with the full knowledge of what prayer is, what an encouragement its promises are, and what its related topics include, our imperfections are such that we still have need of further assistance in the exercise itself. There are two answers to the request, "*Lord teach us to pray*" (Luke 11:1): first, the Lord's prayer (Luke 11:2-4), and second, the promise of the Spirit's help – "*Likewise the Spirit also helpeth our infirmities: for we know not what we should pray for as we ought*" (Rom. 8:26).

If men in an unconverted state do not pray, it is because of the hardness and blindness of their hearts. The Spirit, knowing this to be so, quickens the heart and shines into the soul like the unclouded sun when he arises from the bosom of the morning, and then the soul is laid bare of its contents. The sinner is astonished at what he sees; he beholds its secret chambers full of an uncleanness he scarcely ever dreamed had been slumbering there. He finds himself guilty of ingratitude towards God and he feels himself burdened with a neglect of duty in refusing to love and serve God that weighs him down to the lowest depth. As before he could not pray, now as an awakened sinner he cannot restrain prayer. Can the man who feels himself sinking in the deep waters refrain from crying out for deliverance from the flood? No more can the sinner, enlightened and quickened by the Spirit to see and feel his sin and danger, restrain the prayer that bursts from the heart to the God of his salvation. He calls out as one that must have help and have it instantly. He feels it is now or never!

And if this be the case upon conviction and conversion, it is likewise true in all the subsequent experiences of the believer. He never comes to a time when he can get along without the aid of the Holy Spirit as Prompter, Teacher, and Advocate. Quick as thought, the desires of the petitioner ascend to the throne of grace and glory and in the same instant comes back the gracious assurance, "*I will instruct thee and teach thee in the way which thou shalt go; I will guide thee with mine eye.*" (Ps. 32:8).

If we very earnestly seek His aid, the Holy Spirit will teach us to pray. He will not, it is true, change our mental endowments and give us a different set of faculties. He will not give correctness of grammar to him who has neglected its study and He will not add the amenities of oratory to him who has never acquired them but He *will* quicken the spirit and temper of the mind and assist us in the use of the faculties we already possess. He will give the eloquence of deep feeling, the fire of persistent faith, the warmth of divine love, and the directness of purpose with which a hungry child comes to his mother and asks for bread. The Holy Spirit will teach faith, hope, and love, what to ask for to meet the soul's spiritual thirst and hunger, and how to ask it in the terms of that language which has already been acquired. A child will pray in the words of a child while a man will use words that have some connection with his calling: a statesman in the words of Webster, a conqueror in the words of Cromwell, a scientist in the words of Einstein, and a poet in the words of Milton. To expect anything else would be to look for uniformity where it is expressly said that there shall be diversity; however in *"all these worketh that one and the selfsame Spirit"* (1 Cor. 12:11).

The Spirit *"maketh intercession for the saints according to the will of God."* (Rom. 8:27). He does not make a new revelation of truth but interprets the one already made. We must therefore turn to the law and the testimony and study the revealed will of God. We need not know more than it contains, and we cannot know less, in order to be saved. We are warranted in pleading by its sanctions and making it the basis of our appeal to God. We would not ask what it does not promise. And in a mind under His influence there is not a desire to ask anything beyond the written Word. It contains everything that is needed and sought. Grant what is promised here and we wish for no more. Within that divine record, we find everything we long for, as well in time as in eternity.

And so the whole Word of God becomes of use to direct us in prayer. The study of the Word illustrates the glorious attributes of God and our various relations to Him. *"The words of the Lord are pure words: as silver tried in a furnace of earth, purified seven times."* (Ps. 12:6). *"This is my comfort in my afflictions: for Thy Word hath quickened me."* (Ps. 119:50). *"I delight in Thy law."* (Ps. 119:70b). *"The law of Thy mouth is better unto me than thousands of gold and silver."* (Ps. 119:72). *"O how love I Thy law! it is my meditation all the day."* (Ps. 119:97). The study of the whole Word will show our dependence upon God for life, breath, and continuance, our privileges under grace, and the extent of our obligations to reverently love and obediently serve Him now and forever. In the fair lines of His Word, we read the inspired utterances of His will *"and this is the confidence we have in Him, that if we ask anything according to His will, He heareth us"* (1 John 5:14).

It would be wise and well, therefore, to commit many of its passages to memory. F. W. Robertson used to have an open Bible before him, committing portions of it to memory, while he was dressing in the morning. Thus he redeemed the time, enriched his memory, and gave the Word of God precedence in all the thoughts of the day. But all have not equal facility in the use of memory and for some it has been found beneficial to follow a particular method. Those who have tried it recommend something like this, and there is no doubt but its practice will fix any passage indelibly within the power of recollection. Choose a passage, write it in a blank book procured for this purpose, and read it fifteen times each day for fifteen days in succession; at the end of this time choose another and continue its repetition in the same way for the same length of time and along with it the passage that has already been committed once each day in the way of review. Continue adding a new text and reviewing the preceding texts until twenty-five have been reached; at this stage, as each new text is added the one at the head is dropped and ever after this the number is kept at twenty-five – the first twenty-four of which will be recited but once each day in the way of review and the twenty-fifth fifteen times by way of committal. By this method, twenty-four choice passages of Scripture will be firmly fixed in the mind each year and with the lapse of time will constitute a rich and increasing treasury of spiritual knowledge. Furthermore, by thus becoming familiar with the language of inspiration, our thoughts will be quickened, our imagination will be stimulated to rise on the wings of faith and love, and our petitions, moving in the very atmosphere of inspiration, will become freer and purer from those imperfections which too often mars them.

The following is an authentic story to illustrate the effect of Biblical language upon prayer, coming from where it might be least expected: "I knew a woman who came from the South so illiterate that she could not talk better than an immigrant, though a white woman, but when she began to pray, after a very little while her spirit came to her, she seemed to drop the mortal part, and she fell into the language of the Old Testament. An eminent lawyer said of her that he had heard all the able men in the West but he had never heard a human being that affected him as that poor woman did when she got into those higher moods and brought to her higher nature the use of all that sublime language of the Old Testament that seemed to be congenial to her human nature."

The study of the prayers to be found in the Bible and an endeavor to understand the conditions out of which they arose as urgent desires to God will assist in prayer and serve to bring out the revealed will of God for our guidance under the same needs and circumstances. References to these prayers of the Bible are found at the close of Chapter 10 and I refer the reader to these for his more particular direction and study.

But the more special rule of direction is that form of prayer which Christ taught His disciples, commonly called "The Lord's Prayer." The marvel of this prayer, apart from its beauty and simplicity, is its brevity and comprehensiveness. It has condensed into its few petitions some of the most important truths of the Scriptures. It would almost seem as if the whole Bible had been placed in a solution to form this rarest, fairest, and most radiant of all gems. Like a diamond, it takes the light from all the Scriptures and reflects their truth with a beauty that is all its own and unrivalled. This is a composition that is exclusively divine and is absolutely above criticism. If its petitions were realized for a single day, we should have a heaven on earth and in the morning papers all around the globe we should find nothing to read that would not fully accord with the happy song of the advent angel, "Glory to God in the highest, and on earth peace, good will toward men." (Luke 2:14).

The following suggestive outline has been made of the Lord's prayer (Matt. 6:9-13), which serves to bring its method and important truths into bold relief:

An Invocation: "Our Father, which art in heaven."

Six Petitions: three of which have reference to the glory of God and three to our temporal and spiritual wants:

To the glory of God:
1. "Hallowed be Thy name."
2. "Thy kingdom come."
3. "Thy will be done on earth as it is in heaven."

To our own wants:
1. "Give us this day our daily bread."
2. "And forgive us our debts as we forgive our debtors."
3. "And lead us not into temptation, but deliver us from evil."

A Doxology: "For Thine is the kingdom, and the power, and the glory forever. Amen."

In this the perfections of God are acknowledged and presented as a reason why the prayer should be granted.

And thus the Holy Spirit uses the whole Word of God and whatever in it that is especially relevant to direct and instruct us in prayer. If we depend upon Him, He will assist us in those parts of prayer which consist of invocation, adoration, confession, petition, pleading, dedication, thanksgiving, and blessing; and if prayer in the closet and the family becomes the habit of our life, when our voice shall be lifted up to pray in public it will not sound strange in our ears and prove mere words of the mouth but rather those which have their source in the heart. Have a purpose in your prayer, something to ask for, something to rejoice over, and something to give thanks for. Be assured of this one thing – the graces of grammar and the charms of rhetoric will not so commend our petitions and speed them in their upward flight to the throne of grace; as sincerity, faith, love, hope, humility, a contrite heart, and a broken spirit.

Chapter 19

The Service of Song

In a previous chapter, we have said all that needs to be said about the importance of having good singing in the prayer-meeting. As Horace Greeley used to say, "The only way to resume is to resume," so about singing we would say, the only way to have good singing is to have good singing.

Singing is a language of the emotions, as speech is of the intellect. Song is composed of two parts – the poem and the melody – both conceived in the highest style of art. The first part consists of deep feeling, expressing itself in that variety of composition called poetry. which in all ages has been esteemed the most perfect form of human composition. Because the poet is a genius of old it has been said, "The poet is born, not made." Poetry is thought expressing itself in beautiful language, in beautiful imagery, and in measured cadences and comes from a heart as charged with feeling as an active volcano with fire. There is nothing manufactured about it; it is spontaneous and original.

The other part of song is music, a form of composition for vocal utterance that is likewise conceived in the highest style of perfection. Let us put the two together and what ought not the effect to be upon the hearts of a worshipping people where the sentiment of the song is fully appreciated and its utterance is so expressed as to be correctly given? Let all in the room participate in the exercise and will not such reinforcement fill and shake the whole place with its volume of vocal harmony? What means the fable of Orpheus, or what that nursery ballad of "Over the hills and far away," if not to express the inimitable power of melody? And what will not that power become when song is expressing the loftiest themes of earth and heaven, of time and eternity, as vocalized by victorious hearts sweetly tuned to the same key by the grace of God that bringeth salvation? Some people have been inclined to ridicule the idea that there is so much singing in heaven but that vanishes away when we enter into *"The secret of the Lord"* (Ps. 25:14) and understand what sanctified song is meant to be. Shall not the language of heaven exceed the language of earth? Singing is none other than the language of heaven – the perfection of art in thought and melodious utterance blossoming into the perfect language of heaven. But how are people going to converse in this choice language of heaven if they acquire no ear and voice for the service of song here below? There are so many who have neglected to cultivate their voices here till they are too old to kindle the vocal fires and we may well ask, "What shall these do in heaven?" I have heard it claimed that there are some who are so constituted that they never can learn to sing but Dr. Lowell Mason used to say that anyone who could speak could be instructed to sing.

But however that may be as relates to earth, it will not be so in heaven. The body is to be *"raised in power"* (1 Cor. 15:43) and that includes the voice. On earth, the gifts of voice have been so sparingly distributed that the few who possess them set people wild with the enthusiasm of delight. But even so, the kind and range of these gifted voices are limited within two or three octaves. A bass voice is not a good soprano and a tenor voice is not a good alto. Dr. Mattison, in his work on "The Resurrection of the Body," (Mattison, 1866) carries out the suggestions implied in this promise of God to raise the body *"in power"* (1 Cor. 15:43), perhaps to greater lengths than sober reason would warrant us but no further than Christian hope and a sanctified imagination might safely lead us to anticipate, when he says, "The voice, too, shall be *'raised in power' 'It is sown in weakness, it is raised in power'* (1 Cor. 15:43), not *by* power, but *in* power. They all sing in heaven. The brother who never sang on earth has found a voice there. The Quaker has broken his long silence and the sound of their united voices is *'as the voice of many waters and as the voice of mighty thunderings'* (Rev. 19:6). In the present life the compass of the human voice is but limited. It can be heard but a short distance. It has to be assisted and sustained and the harmony perfected by harps and pianos and organs. It is easily exhausted and finally fails the best vocalists. Now suppose, instead of this, when the body is raised in 'sufficiency,' the range shall be from the highest to the lowest conceivable note, say thirty octaves instead of eight. Suppose, again, it shall be capable of adapting itself to all the different varieties of sounds, like the flute and the horn and the cornet, etc., and shall have power to make itself heard at almost any distance. Then add to this ability to sing one part as well as another or even several parts at once[5] and to sing on without hoarseness or weariness for a day, or a year, or a century! Such, we conceive, would be the human voice 'in power' or 'sufficiency' so that it could express all that the soul can then feel, could vie with the most powerful organ in compass and volume and variety, and dispense forever with all such artificial helps in the immortal praises of our God."

It is a pity that in so many of our churches the congregations should have almost ceased to sing and that the vocal praises of God should be wholly entrusted to a paid choir so that on a Sunday all they have to do is to sit back or stand up to admiringly listen and enjoy the lines at so many dollars a foot. But we hope for better things in the future. In the Sunday-schools almost invariably we have better singing and more of it to the cubic inch than in the church or the prayer-meeting and so we shall look, with such facilities as these afford, for the education of a race of singing Christians who, in the bright and happy days to come, shall fill the house of God, – His courts below – with a volume of unstinted and unpaid melody.

There is always singing talent enough in a church, if we can only bring it into active use. There is less the ability than the disposition. It may be that your people have enjoyed the luxury of a paid choir so long as to have ceased singing the praises of God themselves and, as a result, have come to have neither voice nor heart for it when they assemble in the prayer-meeting. How shall we get them to sing? How again shall we cause the liquid stream of song to flow from their hearts and mouths?

---

5   There was an immigrant boy in the vicinity of New York, in June, 1865, who was able to sing the alto and the soprano of a tune at the same time and Prof. E. Arnold of the Black River Conference, upon seeing this statement in the *New York Christian Advocate*, wrote the author that he had a son who had "a double voice," and could perform the same feat. – Dr. H. Mattison, *of Philadelphia*.

The prayer-meeting is just the place for again opening the gates and refreshing and replenishing the fountains.

The service of song will be greatly improved if we can get the people to come together some twenty minutes before the opening of the prayer-meeting for practice in singing. And even if your people are a singing people, you will find the habit of meeting for an exercise of this sort one of the most pleasant and exhilarating exercises of the whole week. In either case, it will be an excellent preparation for the services to follow and nothing more need be said in favor of this than that it is already a custom with some of the most active churches and wide-awake prayer-meetings in the whole land.

And if directions still more minute ought to be added, we may conclude our chapter with the following suggestions:

First, let the church meet, as has just been said, for vocal practice in song. Let this introduction to the prayer-meeting be social and cheerful. Let the people sit near together and speak freely their likes and dislikes about the pieces that are sung. This will serve to throw off all restraint and prepare the hearts of all for the services to follow.

Second, choose a good hymn-book, with words and music combined if possible, for the use of the prayer-meeting and when it becomes old and time-worn, get a new and better one. A wise rule would be to have a different set for the church, the Sabbath-school, and the prayer-meeting and in their respective places to sing the best in each.

Third, let there be a copy of the hymn-book in each seat so that no one can sit down without having to pick it up. This will deprive all of that trite excuse, "I haven't got a book" and, besides, the progress of a meeting is often disturbed by the people not having the words before them. Let the leader also give directions about the singing. "Mr. Spurgeon comments on the hymns," said Mr. Sankey at the New York Convention, "and tells his congregation how he wants them sung and so the people become deeply interested and there is not a man in his church that is not singing at the top of his voice. If the minister does not manifest any interest in the singing and is studying the heads of his sermon, the choir gets careless and listless. Many a man will come to church and the sermon will pass into and out of his ears and be forgotten but the hymn will linger and work for good. I remember in

Philadelphia, years ago, when I was a little boy, I heard a minister get up and read the hymn, 'There Is a Fountain Filled with Blood.' I have thought of that old man, with his gray hair and tears streaming down his face as he read that hymn, ever since though I have forgotten the sermon and everything else."

Fourth, ask the people to come with one or two hymns in mind that they would like sung that night and if they bring ten times the number that can be sung on any evening, the service will lose nothing thereby but prove all the more exhilarating. By this practice, too, the leader will be kept from revolving in the orbit of his own list of favorite hymns and, besides, through the requisition and use of hymns dear to all the church, a richer variety will be introduced into the song-service of the prayer-meeting than would otherwise be obtained.

Fifth (which ought, perhaps, to stand first), "If you have in your congregation a Christian man who is a good singer," says Mr. Sankey, "I would have him lead the singing. I would have him at the prayer-meeting. Very often some very good man, and sometimes a very good woman, will start up a song entirely out of tune and out of pitch[6] so that no one can join with them and they worry through it, nearly breaking their voice. I would take control of this and say, 'Now Brother Smith or Brother Jones will have charge of the singing and if Brother Smith wants to sit and have one or two friends gathered about him, all the better, and let him pitch the tune. In regard to an instrument at the prayer-meeting, some are opposed to it and some are not. If I had a good singer, one whose voice was strong enough, I would have him instead of an instrument but if not, I would have someone who could play the organ in the proper key and then the people can follow him. I would not always sing all the old tunes we love so well. Of course they are good, but we want variety. Bring in new hymns now and then."

> "Children of the heavenly King!
> As ye journey, sweetly sing;
> Sing your Saviour's worthy praise,
> Glorious in His works and ways."

---

[6] Mistakes of this kind sometimes occur that are quite amusing; as, for instance, when a good deacon and honest man twice started the line, "I love to steal," (from the hymn, "I Love to Steal a While Away")on the wrong tune, tried to get it right, but had to stop at last with the full emphasis on the word "steal."

Chapter 20

How to Secure Attendance

In many of our churches there is the largest attendance on Sunday morning and the evening service is left to take care of itself. The prayer-meeting in the main room of the church would simply be lost and the leader would have to take a lantern in order to hunt up the people and find where to stand while conducting the exercises.

This statement is as true for England as for America. Let us offer as evidence this testimony. "How are the prayer-meetings almost universally neglected?" says Spurgeon of England. "Our own church stands out like an almost solitary green islet in the midst of a dark, dark sea; one bright pearl in the depths of an ocean of discord and confusion. Look at the neighboring churches. Step into the vestry and see a smaller band of people than you would like to think of assembled around the pastor whose heart is dull and heavy. Hear one brother after another pour out the dull, monotonous prayer that he has said by heart these fifty years and then go away and say, 'Where is the spirit of prayer, where the life of devotion?' Is it not almost extinct? Are not our churches 'fallen, fallen, fallen from their high estate?' God, wake them up and send them more earnest and praying men!"

But, if it is the duty of the pastor to preach on Sabbath evenings, is it not the duty of the church to attend? Is there more room than they can fill? Then why did they build the church too large? If it is the duty of the church to have a prayer-meeting, is it not the duty of all the church members to attend and do their best to make it as successful as possible?

In a few churches, very happily, there are found the *"sons of thunder"* (Mark 3:17) to fill them with their eloquence and the question with them is not how to make the people attend but how to let them in and make room for them. Now these men of fire will stay around the gilded rods of the highest steeples and those who live in provincial towns, on the heath, or in the backwoods, need not look for such displays to fill their houses. Let them accept the situation and be content with such good men as the Lord shall be pleased to send them. The people are not helpless; if they will only set to work. What is to prevent them from filling the lecture-room and the church on every occasion? There is nothing at all. *"Let us go up at once, and possess it; for we are well able to overcome it."* (Num. 13:30). In God's name and with God's help, let us hold and occupy the field. If eloquence is lacking, if fine music is lacking, let us fall back upon the good old Gospel and our own duties under it. But be well assured, if you allow one-half or one-third of the church to perform all the duties of the church, there is but a small blessing in store for your church. *"Curse ye Meroz, said the angel of the Lord, curse ye bitterly the inhabitants thereof; because they came not to the help of the Lord, to the help of the Lord against the mighty."* (Judg. 5:23).

If we cannot make the evening attendance for the church and the prayer-meeting a self-executing privilege, let us bring it into the domain of duty. With this end in view, let the people pledge themselves to attend. Let a covenant be prepared to emphasize the importance of a full attendance in such terms as shall meet the necessities of the case and then let some judicious persons take it around among the people for signatures. After these have been secured, the pastor can have the pledge printed on a card and a copy returned to each signer with a brief letter exhorting each to keep in mind what has been pledged and to seek divine guidance in its full performance.

Let us sketch an outline of such a pledge:

> We, the undersigned, do each and severally covenant together, that the work of God may not suffer from our neglect; to faithfully, regularly, and punctually attend all the public services of the church on Sabbath morning and evening and also especially the meeting for prayer on the

week-day evening. We agree that the only excuses for non-attendance shall be such as will approve themselves to our conscience at the time and as we trust will pass inspection on the great review day above.

We also promise to study the topic for the prayer-meeting and take such part in its social worship as our duty shall indicate. We are God's witnesses and as such we desire to speak and pray that eventually our duty may prove a pleasure and participation more a privilege than an unwelcome burden. But whether we take part or not, we will not forsake *"the assembling of ourselves together"* (Heb. 10:25), as has been the manner of some from the beginning, unless unavoidable circumstances prevent us from meeting with the brethren in public assembly.

We also promise that we will not only come ourselves but also by the grace of God helping us, we will invite and endeavor to bring others with us, that thus the rooms of the church may be filled and the rich blessings of God's love and mercy may be as widely distributed in our community as possible (Rev. 22:17).

And we also promise that if we are absent from any stated meeting, we shall always be ready to speak to our pastor or our brethren in the Lord about such absence and that any inquiry into our excuses by them shall not give us offence but be thankfully received by us and esteemed one of the means whereby to provoke unto love and good works.

All this we covenant and agree in the sight of God, who reads our hearts and will approve or condemn our motives according as He sees them to be sincere or not.

Signed, _____

In this matter we need to carry the standard pretty well up to the front. And no one need doubt but that such faithfulness in the discharge of duties as this would secure among all the members, would soon fill the church and wonderfully stimulate the Christian zeal of all in a community.

In one of the fierce battles in the South, so it is related, a colored soldier stood with the banner well up in the front. An officer, fearing that the ensign would be captured, cried out in the thick of the fight, "Come back with that flag!"

"Massa, cap' n," the dusky hero replied, "this heah flag never go back; bring up dem men dar!" "Dem men dar" (those men there) came up to the support of their colors and turned the tide of defeat into a well-earned victory.

My Christian brother, carry the standard well up to the front and then bring up those non-attending and nomadic members from the fields, the woods, and the rear, into rank and file around the uplifted standard of the Cross – who has ever rallied round an ensign more glorious and inspiring? – and the tide of battle will be successfully turned into a victory for every church that is now feeble and despondent. Come to the prayer-meeting whether you take part or not. There may be sufficient reason for your silence but you can always speak by your presence. To be always at the prayer-meeting is an action as eloquent as any speech.

Let church attendance be the last active outdoor duty from which you will retire. Have a resolute mind and an unconquerable spirit and you will live all the longer for such activity and what is more, you will enjoy your old age and we shall hear little about your influence being lost and you yourself laid on the shelf. Old age need not and should not come to you to wither up your faculties and make your days long and wearisome. In attendance on the prayer-meeting, be as strong and tough as old hickory.

Just here, we happen to know what can be done if there be first a willing and decisive mind. We know an entire family that for two years lived six miles from church and yet they regularly attended the prayer-meeting, driving twelve miles to do so, in summer as in winter, in the moonlight as in darkness, over a dangerous road. But you live six blocks from church and call it far! Simeon and Anna, when we read of them in Luke 2, were very old, yet their daily attendance on the temple at morning and evening sacrifice ceased not on that account. Simeon doubtless found it a trial on his strength to go up the hill to the top of Moriah where stood the glorious temple of God and it may be that Anna found it a sort of self-denial to continue in the temple, *"serving God with fastings and prayers night and day."* (Luke 2:37) but oh how precious was their reward! Ere they withdrew from active life, they were both permitted to see the Lord's Anointed, to hold Him lovingly in their arms, and to speak of Him *"to all them that looked for redemption in Jerusalem."* (Luke 2:38).

There are many in our churches – and it is delightful to see them – who are as regular as the seasons in attendance upon the public services of God's house. They have a place there and are always in it irrespective of the weather – may their tribe increase. If you look for them in their place and see them not, you are either growing blind or something like a landslide has taken place between their house and the church.

And perhaps it will not be out of place to give just one instance of the working of the pledge for church and prayer-meeting attendance. It is done with no intention of finding fault with the church that originated the method but rather to hold them up as an example of great wisdom and, under the circumstances, to praise them for the important discovery they have made. The Calvary Presbyterian Church of Springfield, MO, is the leading church in its Presbytery and well-known for its labors of love and self-sacrifice but its members had fallen into the habit so common in all our city churches – that of absenting themselves from the evening services in considerable numbers. Their pastor-elect, in his view of the case, felt it to be his duty to resign. But the church would not permit this and especially so when they learned the reason. They called a meeting of the congregation and immediately applied a remedy for non-attendance in the shape of a pledge which was drawn up and signed. It was handed to the pastor, and of course the ground of his action was removed. He then prefixed a letter to the pledge and had both printed together on a card so that a copy might be sent to each one of the original signers. The following is a literal copy of that card:

"Brethren, be not weary in well-doing."

*Dear*_____,

The following Pledge was handed to me with your name signed to it. The good Lord is pleased with our vows made to Him, when He sees us earnestly trying to keep them. Believing that a frequent reading of this solemn Pledge to which you have subscribed your name will assist you to carry it out, I herewith send you a copy of it. Please read Psalm 66:12; Psalm 76:11; Psalm 116:14.

                  Your Pastor,
                  C. H. DUNLAP.

PLEDGE

We now pledge ourselves to self-examination and prayer, that the Holy Spirit may come into our hearts, to seek His enlightening power, that we may see our duty as believers, and to impart to us such a sense of our obligations to our Lord as will enable us to engage heartily in all Christian work, by a more regular attendance upon all the services of the sanctuary, by the cultivation of the grace of benevolence, and by seeking such a spirit of love to all that we shall set a watch upon our lips and hearts, that all evil speaking, with all bitterness, may be put away from us.

"Forsake not the assembling of yourselves together."

"Whatsoever thy hand findeth to do, do it with thy might."

"Lo! I am with you always."

So far as we know, the result of this action has come up to their most optimistic expectations. The evening services were at once well attended, the pastor was greatly encouraged – for to preach to slim audiences in the evening is the severest trial of the pastor's duty, the people were delighted by the new tokens of refreshing from the presence of the Lord, and with increased hopefulness the work began to go forward in their midst. Both pastor and people are entitled to honorable mention for having so happily and harmoniously solved the difficulty and their discovery is one that should not be lost to the church at large. *"Examine yourselves, whether ye be in the faith; prove your own selves, . . . how that Jesus Christ is in you, except ye be reprobates?"* (2 Cor.13:5).

And, when all this has been accomplished, it ought to be said, "Do not let attendance upon the prayer-meeting remain in the domain of duty." While it is a duty, let us, as soon as that has been recognized and a full attendance secured, make everything connected with the prayer-meeting so bright, cheerful, and attractive that our people shall never think of the duty but only of the pleasure and profit that regular attendance produces. To this end, pastor and people should bend their energy and employ every useful and upright method. One of these, among others, will be found in the practice of the people to invite and bring with them to the prayer-meeting their company, whether visitors or guests, and also in the endeavor to bring distinguished strangers to the meeting who, when they visit the town, shall be kindly invited by the pastor or any of the people to come and take part in the exercises of the evening. And in fact, for that matter, strangers should always be invited and made welcome whether they can take part or not. Their mere presence will be encouraging.

A continued concern like this on the part of the whole church will be sure to keep up the interest in the meetings and make them ready to discover honorable means by which to increase their influence and power for good. There is no merit in making people attend from a sheer sense of duty.

Chapter 21

How Prayer-Meetings are kept at a White Heat

"How are prayer-meetings kept at a white heat?"
– *Correspondent.*

To answer the above question in a very practical way, we assigned a ministerial reporter to visit several of the most successful prayer-meetings in New York and Brooklyn. We share the following from his note-book:

At the Fulton Street noonday prayer-meeting, which has met every business day at noon for the past twenty years, we found in attendance about one hundred people, mostly business men. The meeting began punctually at one o'clock to the minute. No speech or prayer was allowed to exceed five minutes. A portion of Scripture, carefully prepared by a previously appointed leader, was read and commented on very briefly and pointedly. Requests for prayer, twenty or thirty, were read from the desk while others were made verbally by speakers. Prayers were earnest. Every minute was occupied. No loud talking, noise, or excitement but the deepest kind of earnestness was manifested. The assembly had the appearance of a meeting of a lot of earnest business men who had come together to talk over some vital business matter. The leading spirits of this meeting are men of conviction; men who are as sure God answers prayer as they are that the sun is shining above the clouds at noon today. Promptness, eagerness, earnestness, common business sense applied to religion, faith, and the consequent presence of the Spirit of God keep this meeting at "white heat."

The prayer-meeting at the Brooklyn tabernacle is, perhaps, more largely attended than any other in the world. We found about two thousand people in attendance; it was a threefold meeting and lasts from 7:30 to 9:15. The first half hour is spent in congregational singing.[7] (This church has no choir but is led in its singing by the organ and a song leader.) From 8:00-8:30, Dr. Talmage delivers a prepared and, to his audience, an exceedingly interesting "review of the secular events of the week from a religious standpoint." This review is gotten up in a popular lecture style and helps to draw the crowds. At the conclusion of the lecture, the audience has permission to retire or remain for the actual prayer-meeting. The lecture bait has evidently caught many. Curiosity is excited, so the larger proportion of the great audience remains. Dr. Talmage takes his seat on the front of the platform and calls upon some brother, who has the gift to make a brief, earnest, sympathetic prayer, to pray. The leader keeps the reins well in hand: "I would like to take testimony tonight whether Christianity is true or not. The Bible says that those who are faithful Christians will know that Christianity is true. There are those here whom you know to be honest men; men who would scorn to bear false testimony. They have been Christians for twenty, thirty, fifty years. Now, what say they? Do they know by experience that Christianity is a truth? You would take their testimony on any other matter. There is no judge in this city who would not deem them capable witnesses. Here is a matter of which they say they have positive knowledge. They are capable witnesses." One after another of aged Christians was called upon to bear testimony concerning his experimental knowledge of the truth of the religion of Jesus. Younger men testified. Brief exhortations by the pastor and others, in the same line of thought, followed. Prayers, pointed and brief, were

---

7   The prayer circle of Dr. Kittredge's church in Chicago meets fifteen minutes before the prayer-meeting to spend the time in social song. They sing without the aid of an instrument and by the time their prayer-meeting opens they have all been stirred up by the melodies they have sung and lifted up in spirit to enter with zest into the services of prayer, praise, and exhortation that follow.

made for the immediate conversion of the unconverted present. Then, those desiring the prayers of God's people were requested to stand up. Fifty or more arose. After an earnest prayer by the pastor, the meeting adjourned. The actual prayer-meeting lasted three-quarters of an hour.

Here also they have found the secret of keeping a prayer-meeting at "white heat."

– *Metropolitan Pulpit.*

Chapter 22

Treatment of the Monthly Concert

The Gospel needs of the world are so great and important that a place for their consideration ought to be given them in the scheme of topics. Now it is so well known that the monthly concert for missions will be a dry presentation of facts and figures that people more readily stay away on those evenings than any other. We have only to improve this treatment and make it pleasing, as well as instructive, in order to arouse the attention of the church and secure a fuller attendance.

We have already alluded to a general plan by which the concert can be made more interesting than it usually is, but some additional particulars may here be specified which shall give a growing interest to the monthly presentation of the missionary subject.

The concert should be made the occasion for the study of history. I suppose none of us know very much about the history of lands other than our own. Each month we have a particular field of the world under review. Let us investigate certain subjects connected with the history of that portion of the world such as its language, literature, religion, social condition, and political relations.

Let us take India, for example. We may profitably study from year to year such subjects as these: The history of India from the earliest times, the importance of the discovery of the new route to India by the Cape of Good Hope, the chartering of the East India Company by Queen Elizabeth, the license granted to this company by the Great Mogul to establish a trading-post in India, Lord Clive and the conquest of India, the steps by which this populous and extended region was opened for the Gospel, the rule of the East India Company, the impeachment of Warren Hastings, the struggle over the renewal of charter in 1813, the Crimean War and its results, the Sepoy Rebellion, the extinction of the Company's rule and the elevation of Victoria as sovereign of India in 1858, her elevation to be Empress of India in 1877, the civilization of India under British rule, the labors of this and that missionary in India, etc.

Nor will it be out of place to devote time to the study of geography in its two branches of physical and descriptive – the climate and the products of the soil in their relation to civilization and religion, such as hindrances in the way of civilizing Africa from its climate and the explorations and discoveries of Livingstone and Stanley in Africa – physical geography as modified by human action. Thus in China, at the present, the lamentable famine by which thousands are perishing has been caused by the destruction of the forests in that sadly stricken region. In former times, the hills which fringe that vast plateau, now the seat of famine, were covered with thick woods. They have been entirely cleared. From Peking to Hankow, a distance of 700 miles, scarcely a tree or shrub is to be seen. As a result of such wasteful destruction, 70,000,000 of the people in this thickly settled region are in want of food and some 9,000,000 of them are actually starving. This is a lesson that should not be lost on the people of the United States. Such remarks as it may be proper to make on the geography of a country will be rendered all the more instructive if reinforced by references to a good map, hanging in such position as to be readily seen by all in the room. With a graphic oral presentation of physical characteristics and the like, we can more readily imagine ourselves in those countries where our missionaries are laboring and see the peculiar helps or hindrances by which they may be surrounded. In this way, too, we shall more readily discover the importance of the field and its various relations to the world at large.

Again, the concert will give excellent opportunity for the study of comparative religion. There are about a dozen different religions of mankind. What are the distinctive features of each? Five of these, for example, are found in India – Christianity, Brahmanism, Mohammedanism, Buddhism, and Parseeism. The three essentially missionary religions of the world – Christianity, Mohammedanism and Buddhism – are here confronting each other and struggling for supremacy. What will be the result? By methods of research like these, we shall become better acquainted with the moral condition of the great unchristian world and the churches will be progressively enlightened about its immediate and pressing needs.

And finally, a brief presentation of what is being accomplished yearly in each field will be useful to awaken an interest and give it intelligent direction and from such knowledge of struggles and hindrances, defeats and triumphs, hopes and encouragements, the church will learn better both how to pray and how to contribute.

The annual recurrence of the same missionary fields should not call for a repetition of the same thoughts but should afford the occasion for the progressive presentation of new lines of research in history, religion, geography, government, and achievements. To revive a missionary zeal in the churches, we need only to pour in a flood of light upon these subjects[8] and as a result, under the divine blessing, such a prayerful interest will be maintained in the world-wide diffusion of the Gospel as shall advance the cause of truth both at home and abroad.

> "Watchman, tell me does the morning
>   Of fair Zion's glory dawn;
> Have the signs that mark His coming
>   Yet upon my pathway shone?
> Pilgrim, yes, arise, look round thee,
>   Light is breaking in the skies;
> Spurn the unbelief that bound thee
>   Morning dawns, arise, arise!"

---

[8] As an aid in this direction, each church ought to own a missionary library more or less complete that should be accessible to the membership in preparing for the Monthly Missionary Concert.

Chapter 23

Laying out Work

It has been claimed by an English clergyman, J. Service, that the church of today has lost its early, practical character and hence fails to accomplish her full work. He objects that it is all preaching and no work. "The kind of meeting to which this pointed (Heb. 10:24-25) was a meeting in which everybody who chose to had a voice, in which everybody who had any advice or information or exhortation to give was free to give and was expected to give it." "*To provoke unto love and to good works,*" to "*consider one another,*" to take steps for the relief of their poor, the succor of their sick, the instruction of the young, the conversion of their heathen friends, the advancement of their faith, the promotion of every scheme which an enthusiastic philanthropy suggested for making the world better and happier – this was the business which brought them together. They did not meet as we do, to sing psalms, pray and hear a sermon, and go away home till next Sunday. Their meetings did not end as ours regularly and systematically do, in nothing at all. And so, he reasons, we ought to introduce a more popular and practical element into our service.

"If we were united," he goes on to say, "in the loosest sort of way – united as a congregation in an endeavor to further Christian objects, to relieve the poor, to comfort the sick, to instruct the ignorant, to reclaim the erring, to remove temptation out of the way of the young, to promote decency, sobriety, honesty, truth, gentleness – if we were ever so loosely united as a congregation in this endeavor, it is impossible, being as many as we are, that we should not accomplish something. Now if there were this kind of business first and devotion followed or if business and devotion were somehow combined in the order of our Sunday services, we should have what gives zest to meetings for other and inferior purposes – the sense that we are dealing with what is immediate and of practical utility to ourselves and others. Were we able to report today that some work for the poor, or the sick, or the ignorant, or the tempted, had been done by us since last Sunday, or had we now met to spend part of our time in considering what work of that kind might be attempted by us this week, I need not say our meeting would be more lively, for one thing, than our meetings usually are and not the least so in respect of our devotion. In carrying on our work, the practical and useful would come to the aid of devotion, devotion would aid work, we would meet difficulties and pray the better on account of them, we would have some success and because of it sing a more hearty song." This, he contends, was the purpose for which the early Christians came together on the first day of the week, and this was the nature of their worship – a meeting in which all had a voice for the transaction of business, for reporting what had been done, and for suggesting what might be done on the coming week and hence they were so successful and grew in number so rapidly.

Now this criticism might be more applicable to a church which holds no week-day meetings for fellowship, prayer, and exhortation, without a Sabbath-school, and with a changing congregation. We are thankful to receive every suggestion that might aid a church to do more than it is doing for Christ and humanity – and there is probably no church but might do a little more than it is doing – but with the various meetings and schools which we have, there is less occasion for any change in the order and nature of our public services on the Sabbath. The church is a continuous organization and does not pass out of existence when her members go home to dine or when the doors are closed at night for another week. And there is not so much change in the congregation either, except in the larger cities, so that the great majority of our churches are continuous organizations for work. We have the Sabbath-school for instruction and a more intimate acquaintance with the facts and principles of the Bible. There remains, then, a need for just such pulpit ministrations as are now given on the Lord's Day that thus the Spirit of God may make the preaching of the Word an effectual means of convincing and converting sinners and of building them up in holiness and comfort through faith unto salvation.

In some churches there are industrial schools where the young are regularly instructed in certain departments of home work, in neatness and cleanliness, and when cases of want and distress occur, they are looked after and relieved and not only kind words are spoken but also something to wear is given.

In most churches the ladies meet weekly from house to house for prayer and fellowship. The neighbors are invited in to participate and in this way strangers are reached and new opportunities for doing good are discovered. And then there are the weekly prayer-meetings of the church which present abundant opportunity for doing just such a work, or planning for it, as was suggested for the Sunday service, and which, it seems to us, is more appropriate for such a time and meeting.

We might, perhaps, with great advantage to ourselves, introduce this feature into our prayer-meetings for a few minutes, or so many as should be needed for this purpose, towards the close of the meeting in which members might report what Christian work they had done or were doing (whether they had been helpful to any or had tried to be), to relieve the poor, to comfort the sick, to reclaim the erring, to remove temptation from the young, to promote the many good works for lack of which humanity lies suffering and bleeding, and to suggest what might be done while the week is still in progress, for in all these respects the church may prove herself a power for good in every community and a fountain from which shall flow streams of blessing, sweetness, and kindness. But in recounting work of this kind it would be very needful – and one cannot be too careful – to avoid the Pharisaic spirit as illustrated by the parable of the Pharisee and the Publican in Luke 18:9-14. Thus, when the Christian is eaten up with zeal for the Lord's house and the Lord's work, he will run to and fro on the Lord's business and esteem the service a gladsome privilege.

There are also other branches for usefulness in the machinery of the church – wheels within wheels – such as missionary bands, societies, and officers in the church. These are set as watchmen upon the walls of our church that they may more readily discern what is useful and needful to do and to be done. We cannot, then, with so many arms and hands for work, complain of their lack but rather of our failure to reach them out in as many helpful directions as the suffering needs of humanity require. Yes, the church is an organization for work. We are to be helpful to one another both spiritually and temporally. The church is the grandest of all organizations because it is the body of Christ and if there is any society that claims to be useful, the church should be all that it claims and more too.

We should have a watchful interest in each other – especially in the children and youth of the congregation – and ever seek to improve them, ever seek to help them in honorable and needful ways so that they may be able to help themselves and in their turn become able to help others. When anyone is out of employment and in need of place and work, we should be ready with kind words, hopeful sympathy, and actual solicitation in their behalf. The true economy of life is to help others in such a way that they can help themselves. It is not so much charity they need as work and compensation.

Now it may be easier to send your money to the heathen and delegate others to do good for you than to take such personal interest in those right around you so that when they are in pressing need, their wants shall receive immediate attention. And so it is reported of a wealthy firm in one of the great cities of the land, the members of which are pillars in a church – whose integrity no man questions – that they had had a man in their service until he became old and sick and, being unable to work, they stopped his salary and he and his family were brought to the verge of starvation. The congregation's attention was called to his condition and a few dollars were sent for his relief but it was a mere mite in contrast with their generous contributions to the charities of their church and had it not been for the aid and sympathy of his fellow-clerks, he would have died and received burial as a pauper. As it was, through the clerk's benevolence, the old man was supported comfortably while he lived and in death received those kindly attentions which the heart loves to bestow on the objects of its care. The giving of large sums of money to a public charity attracts more notice and gains more fame than giving it for the benefit of some poor individual – some Peter, John, or Paul – that has fallen among thieves on the road to Jericho. While so much money is sent to the bushmen of Africa or elsewhere, is there no one to take a personal interest in the tramp on the road to Jericho, the roustabout on a Mississippi steamer, the waif of the street whose home is a dry-goods box, or the orphan that sweeps the crossings and begs a penny from people they pass on, dry-shod and unsoiled? It is so much easier to weep over pictured misery in the South Sea Islands, than shed tears over the shoe-shiner in your own city whose scant earnings may buy bread and butter for some invalid mother or destitute sister. We all need to read and lay to heart the Parable of the Good Samaritan (Luke 10:30-37).

The prayer-meeting will afford excellent opportunity to speak of just such cases as need help, work, and sympathy. But if it be not proper to make such business a part of its exercises, it certainly will not be out of place to spend five or ten minutes after the close of each meeting in social interaction about such charitable work as the church ought to undertake and prosecute. How easy it would be in this way to stimulate a zeal for the thorough visitation of the district in which the church is located in order to discover both the temporal and the spiritual needs of the neighboring community. How easy it would be to create an enthusiasm in works of benevolence if such opportunity were given in connection with the discovery of needs and the comparison of notes. How easy it would be to fill up our churches, our Sabbath-schools, and our prayer-meetings. It is not the ability that we lack as much as the inclination and the zeal. God will give all the grace that such undertakings require as fast as the grace He has already given is used. Look at the zeal of Dwight Moody when a young convert. His first effort was to hire four pews in Plymouth Church, Chicago, and keep them full of young men every Sunday and then, next, to fill up a mission school on the North Side, and he has kept at this business of filling up churches ever since.

> *"Then shall the King say unto them on His right hand,
> Come, ye blessed of my Father, inherit the kingdom prepared
> from the foundation of the world: for I was an hungered and
> ye gave me meat; I was thirsty, and ye gave me drink; I was
> a stranger and ye took me in; naked and ye clothed me; I*

was sick and ye visited me; I was in prison and ye came unto me. Then shall the righteous answer him, saying Lord, when saw we thee an hungered, and fed thee? or thirsty and gave thee drink? When saw we thee a stranger, and took thee in? Or naked and clothed thee? or when saw we thee sick, or in prison, and came unto thee? And the King shall answer and say unto them, Verily I say unto you, inasmuch as ye have done it unto one of the least of these my brethren, ye have done it unto me." (Matt. 25:34-40).

Chapter 24

The Social Element in the Prayer-Meeting

It may be that not enough is made of the social element in our religious life. If it is important to have people sit near together and well up to the front in the prayer-meeting in order to produce a certain feeling of comfort and interest, as everyone knows to be the case, might we not make still more of this principle if we were to tarry for fifteen or thirty minutes after the meeting closed for a general conversation on the subject of the evening? If in the large cities of our land we may have enough or too much of social life, in the country it is generally the case that they have too little. But however that may be, it is true of both that we do not have enough of social life where the inspiration and basis is religious feeling. Life of this kind will find its best culture in connection with labors in the Sabbath-school, with the services of the Sabbath, and the week-day prayer-meeting. And, indeed, I know of no place where the religious cultivation of sociability would be more appropriate and adapted to produce pleasure and improvement than as the outgrowth of the prayer-meeting. Now I would not have conversation of such a nature as to dissipate the religious impressions of the evening but rather of that stimulating kind which shall deepen them and make them more lasting. After an hour of worship, if it has been wide awake and inspiring, feelings are stirred and thoughts suggested for which social interaction would open suitable channels of expression. Sometimes our best thoughts come to us after the meeting is closed and oft times, too, a casual remark is thrown out by one who did not take part in the exercises for that evening that sets the subject in a new and pleasing light.

An illustration of this subject comes to mind. During this last winter, I was invited to lead a historical class composed of some forty or fifty members of our church. This circle was originated by two or three ladies who felt that this would be a delightful way of spending the winter season before us, that it would revive the happy memories of school days, and foster a taste for study and reading that would prove valuable means to promote a lifelong culture. Now there are different ways of reading history; we chose the one best adapted for the purpose we had in view and that was the topical study of history. We used as a basis for our investigations White's "Eighteen Christian Centuries," (White, 1878) or, at least, we depended upon that for a narrative in outline of the leading events in each century and in connection therewith we investigated questions in literature, science, art, invention, discovery, philosophy, church history, etc., that were the most pronounced in each. Well, what I started to write was this: after ten or twelve persons had given the results of their researches upon the topics assigned them, the recitation in history would be closed for the evening and the company would then branch out into a free social conversation on the topics that had been presented or in the interchange of such greetings as the occasion rendered fitting. In groups of three or four, the class would linger for half an hour or so, loath to depart till the lateness of the hour made it imperative. Now I venture to say that the social feature in this historical circle was quite as valuable as the improvement derived from the study of history for it was, perhaps, this very thing that kept the class together for over six months, that gave such seeming importance to the study of history, and kept up an interest in it from week to week without abatement until the hot weather, and not fatigue or boredom, rendered an adjournment judicious.

But do you say, "We don't have time to tarry after the meeting closes?" You have if you want to, for I find we can stay up pretty late if the entertainments we attend are to our relish. People say they cannot go to an evening service of the church or the prayer-meeting for this or that reason, each one so sound and valid as to be unanswerable, but let something come along that they have a curiosity to attend and all their excuses are as easily brushed away as cobwebs by a broom. At such a time, they find plenty of reasons for attending and you could not hire them to stay away if you tried. Our historical class found time to spend two to three hours together every other week besides taking hours between for visiting libraries and hunting up authorities on the subjects. "But," you may say, "those were young people who had nothing else to do." Not so; it is true that the circle included young persons and students but, besides these, there were men and matrons, lawyers and successful business men, all of whom had plenty to occupy their time and energy in the respective spheres of their duty and callings. I say, then, if you have the will, you will find the way for you have all the time there is and no one has more.

For what purposes, then, should we cultivate sociability in connection with the prayer-meeting? We need to be reminded, as has been said, that the prayer-meeting is the development of the social element in religious directions and that with the beginning of the prayer-meeting begins the development of the social feeling. We should strive to bring out, from time to time, a full record of the dealings of God with His household, the church. In the first place, this tends to produce that almost unknown quality of which so much is said in the New Testament and so little is known in the church of the Lord – fellowship: a sort of joyful inspiration at the sense of a fellow by your side, that kind of relation one to another which persons have who meet together on a Thanksgiving or Christmas when the household comes together. Everybody is glad. Nobody can tell why unless it is because my uncle and my aunt and my grandfather, etc. are here. There is that feeling of heart exaltation and persons run around and laugh because they feel so happy. Well, gather a church together and bring them into such relations that all feel that yearning, brotherly feeling and that gladness and exultation in each other. Ah! and you never can do this as long as you set people apart in pens, set them up straight and make it a sin to look at one another, setting them all to thinking about God and holiness, drifting them out of the spheres of ordinary feeling. They come in so proper, put their hats down properly, sit down properly, and nobody speaks above a whisper.

You cannot produce that feeling of fellowship like this. And with such a beginning, it will be hard to give the meeting a cheerful and hopeful turn or pass into anything like sociability when the meeting has closed, for all the way through, they will feel as a father felt when he said to his children on a Sabbath morning, "Take down the Bible and let us have an *awfully* solemn time."

If, on the other hand, we enter into the joyful spirit of Christian fellowship at the very beginning of the meeting, we shall then be ready when it closes, to exchange information about the wants and needs of our community, to speak about the sick, to present cases of destitution that need help, to talk about some whom we ought to assist, and to give the address of strangers who have lately moved into our community and decide who should carry out the Christian duty to call on them for further acquaintance.

We might also exchange views on the topic of the evening and the method of its presentation with such thoughts as have been suggested thereby in our own minds. *"As in water face answereth to face, so the heart of man to man."* (Prov. 27:19).

It may be possible that we are not on as good terms with some as we ought to be; we have become estranged for some reason or other and do not feel very cordial. What place would be better than the prayer-meeting in which to brush away all obstructions of this kind and make the opportunity which the after-meeting would present a sort of reunion and love feast. *"Therefore if thou bring thy gift to the altar, and there rememberest that thy brother hath aught against thee, leave there thy gift before the altar, and go thy way; first be reconciled to thy brother, and then come and offer thy gift."* (Matt. 5:23-24). Do not presume that you can worship God acceptably while there is ill-will and enmity in your heart towards any of your fellow-creatures or unresolved difficulties *"For if ye forgive men their trespasses, your heavenly Father will also forgive you. But if ye forgive not men their trespasses, neither will your Father forgive your trespasses."* (Matt. 6:14-15).

And on the top of this cordial reconciliation with all the brethren, heartfelt greetings would descend like the dew upon Hermon (Ps. 133:3) and words of kindness will flow like oil cast upon the waters of life's troubled sea. Ah! how truly is it said:

> "Kind words can never die,
>   Cherished and blest,
> God knows how deep they lie
>   Stored in the breast;
> Like childhood's simple rhymes
> Said o'er a thousand times,
> Go through all years and climes
>   The heart to cheer."

There is all too much friction in the movement of life's machinery and rivalries. The world is full, all too full, of sadness and suffering! Through how many a heart has driven the ploughshare? Over how many a field has the harrow been dragged? Gentleness and sympathy may not remove the ills of life but who shall estimate the value of the dew and sunshine when spring time has come and the seeds of life's harvest lie slumbering in the soil awaiting an eternal reaping?

Gentleness and sympathy may not entirely remove the burdens, the sadness, and the sufferings that happen in life but they may do much to alleviate them.

> "Teach me to feel another's woe;
>   To hide the fault I see.
> That mercy I to others show,
>   That mercy show to me."

And I doubt not but that such cultivation of kindness and brotherly love would give enlargement to the graces of speech and the amenities of life as well as teach us to shun such gossip as the Scriptures denounce and which has a tendency, not to bind hearts closer in the golden chain of Christian fellowship, but to breed jealousies, rivalries, ill-will, and continual vexation. "*Let your conversation be as becometh the Gospel*" (Phil. 1:27). "*So be ye holy in all manner of conversation*" (1 Pet. 1:15). "*Let your speech be alway with grace, seasoned with salt*" (Col. 4:6). Conversation of this nature, I am sure, would deepen the volume of Christian experience and promote our growth in holiness and the rich graces of the Spirit. And as a result of all this, we should become better and better acquainted with the household of faith and discover, perhaps to our astonishment, with what very amiable people our lot has been cast.

Let us sum it all up in the timely words of another. "Care should be taken to notice strangers and to introduce them, so that when they come again they may feel they are among friends. Every one – the pastor setting the example and leading the way – should take pains and devise methods for cultivating this sociability in the prayer-meeting. It will spread an atmosphere of good feeling which will make such meetings delightful to those who habitually attend and attract others to come to their enjoyment, as well as constitute them to be the very places where the Holy Spirit may most certainly be expected."

Chapter 25

Hints New and Old

The following hints have been selected by way of review and to emphasize some things of chief value to be looked after in the conduct of the prayer-meeting. *"To every man his work"* (Mark 13:34). *"Go work today in my vineyard."* (Matt. 21:28).

Attendance, etc.

1. Arrange your affairs so as to attend the prayer-meeting and be sure to come, unless under the same circumstances you would have to break a social or business engagement.

2. Come yourself. Bring your children. The prayer-meeting is not complete without the children, any more than the family circle.

3. If you are entertaining friends, bring your visitors with you and let the church give them a rousing social welcome after the meeting is closed.

4. Bring some unconverted friend with you and pray for a blessing upon him before the meeting closes.

5. Come early, if possible; if not, come late but by all means come early.

6. Come to the meeting in the spirit of prayer and with the desire to take a part should time and opportunity be given. Those meetings have been the best that have been preceded by the most prayer.

7. Let the seats in front and near the leader be taken first. Sit side by side and if there are to be any vacant chairs, let them be in the rear

of the room. There is no rule for the success of religious meetings that Christians are slower to act upon than this – always to fill the front seats first and closely pack them. It seems a trivial thing but it is a matter of prime importance. What kind of sociability would there be in a house if a dozen guests should sit down each in a room by himself and then try to talk and be social through the doors and across the hall? Scatter the embers and they go out; draw them together and they burn and glow. The fingers in a mitten warm each other; in a glove they are chilled by separation.

8. Never give a concert, lecture, or other entertainment the preference if they come on the same evening as the prayer-meeting. Let the prayer-meeting be first.

9. Study and pray over the topic for the week that you may fill your mind with its precious truth and make the prayer-meeting itself a theme of frequent conversation with your family and friends during the week.

10. Open and close the meeting promptly. If any indulgence is to be made, let it be in favor of a shorter rather than a longer session.

11. Occasionally devote five minutes or so at the close of the meeting for reports on work or new plans for work. There should also be an opportunity given somewhere in every meeting for a man to speak or pray whose heart is full and must find utterance whether he is down on the program or not.

12. Carefully exclude controversy and contradiction. The prayer-meeting is not a debating society.

13. As the weekly prayer-meeting is the gathering together of the household of Christ for growth in grace, for worship, and for mutual sympathy, let all restraint, formality, and criticism be left outside. Don't let them cross the threshold. (See Heb. 4:16.)

14. But if all your efforts to wake up the mind of the church to the importance of prompt and full attendance on the prayer-meeting should fail, introduce the "League and Covenant" for attendance (See Chapter 20) and if that will not secure the hoped-for result, you may conclude that you have sufficient reason as pastor to seek a different field of labor.

Variety

In order not to have any monotony in the exercises from week to week, it would be wise to change them and to a certain extent have the meetings, as they proceed, vary as to their nature. We place here what has previously been given on this topic.

1. Conduct the meeting in the usual way. Custom has endeared it and it may be really valuable.

2. If the topic be suitable, use it as the theme for a Bible reading.

3. Have a set program in which you have a place for one or two old men, for one or two middle-aged men, and for one or two young men who have promised to attend and speak to the topic. Arrange also for two or three to pray for some urgent need of the church and congregation.

4. Announce for the next meeting that everything shall be voluntary and just as soon as the topic has been developed and the supply of participants ceases, stop the meeting though you are but halfway through the hour; at all events, don't run beyond the time.

5. If you have a missionary topic, arrange for the reading of several letters, essays, etc.

6. If the season be suitable, arrange for a praise meeting, a promise meeting, a seed-time meeting, a "harvest-home" meeting, a memorial or "Ebenezer" (1 Sam. 7:12) meeting, and the like.

7. Occasionally have a new leader conduct the meeting. Such variety as this would introduce into the meetings would give life, animation, and interest to them. The people would assemble each time in expectation of something new and would not be disappointed.

Procedure

1. "How is it then, brethren, when ye come together... Let all things be done unto edifying." (1 Cor. 14:26).

2. How can we cherish a sense of the Divine Presence in every meeting? Do we expect Christ to meet with us? How can we secure the aid and cooperation of the Holy Spirit, for without Him our meeting will be in vain and worse than in vain? As aids to an answer, we ought to read, ponder, and pray over such texts of Scripture as these: Hos. 10:12,

Hab. 3:2, Zech. 4:6, Matt. 18:19-20, Mark 1:2-4, Luke 11:9-13, Rom. 8:26-27, Eph. 5:18, and Jas. 5:16. Ought not the prayers, then, at the opening of the meeting to be burdened with petitions that God will hear us and grant us the presence of His Son and His Spirit?

3. Brevity in remarks and prayers is essential both to the interest of the meeting and its prompt dismissal. It is well to have as large a number as possible participate so that, while the exercises have unity, they may not lack variety. Lengthy remarks generally become dull and long prayers are a departure from the models given in the Bible. The prayer of Solomon at the dedication of the temple – perhaps the longest prayer in the Bible – did not occupy much over five minutes (1 Kin. 8:22-53, 2 Chron. 6:12-42). *"But when ye pray, use not vain repetitions as the heathen do: for they think that they shall be heard for their much speaking."* (Matt. 6:7) Experience has shown that from three to five minutes, on an average, is as much time as each one ought to use in taking part and hence an address should make up in quality for what it lacks in quantity. Brevity will require condensation, point, and purpose to our petitions. "I never like to hear one of my people," says Spurgeon, "pray for half an hour and conclude with asking the Lord to forgive our *shortcomings*."

4. When you speak or pray, be sure to speak loud enough for all to hear you.

5. Ought not "scolding" to be carefully avoided? Does it pay to scold those who are present because others are absent? I know of a case where the church was emptied by a minister scolding those who came because others kept away. If things do not go right, take them to the Lord in prayer. That will kindle a fire in the pulpit which will kindle a fire in the pew and make the house comfortable. Praise what is commendable and let us all, in the spirit of Heb. 10:24-25, cultivate a more fervent type of piety.

6. How can we avoid the "long pauses" that drag and spoil a meeting? By each one having something to say or read which he cannot permit the meeting to close without hearing. We ought to be willing to speak for Christ even if we cannot imitate the accent of Cicero or the eloquence of Demosthenes. If we will only tell what we feel, we shall all be eloquent enough and glorify God in a way pleasing to Him.

7. If our hearts are full, we shall hardly be able to wait for our turn. Go to an exchange where stocks are sold and listen to the brokers all bidding at once and learn the secret.

8. In moments of deep solemnity, it is very proper to give a moment or two to silent prayer. At the revival meetings conducted by our dear brethren, Major Whittle and Mr. Bliss, in our city in the fall of 1876, I was much impressed with this custom which they repeatedly used and I am convinced that it did much good. During those moments of silent prayer, the house was so still that you could have heard a pin drop; yes, you could almost have heard your heart beat.

9. Let us enter into the spirit of the meeting. Sing *"with grace in your hearts to the Lord."* (Col. 3:16). Each prayer becomes our own if we follow it understandingly and add to it a silent or audible "amen."

10. Do not wander from the topic and begin a rehash of what you have said before a dozen times or so. A new topic each week allows for new thought, illustration, and experience.

11. Have you no written requests for special prayer to bring to the prayer-meeting? If you have, hand these to the pastor before the meeting. If you have a special object of desire, ask others to join with you in seeking it. *"If two of you shall agree on earth as touching any thing that they shall ask, it shall be done for them of my Father which is in heaven."* (Matt. 18:19) Ask for something. Give thanks for something. Have a point in your prayer.

12. And when you receive the answer to your prayer, do not fail to speak of it for this encourages others to pray and confirms their faith.

13. Is it proper to cultivate the spirit of friendliness? If you are early and notice strangers, seek an introduction or introduce yourself and speak to them in words of welcome. Can you not spend a few minutes after the close of the meeting for hand-shaking and the exchange of greetings with your friends and neighbors? Shake hands with as many as possible and in every proper way cultivate the spirit of sociability. Why are you in such a hurry to go home from the prayer-meeting? Why can't you spend several minutes in conversation about the topic and in suggesting plans for work and greater usefulness? Would not such friendliness as this make the meetings social and delightful and create the feeling that *"it is good for us to be here"* (Matt. 17:4, Mark 9:5, Luke 9:33)?

It will be easy for you to speak a friendly word for Jesus then while the warmth of the meeting is upon you.

14. Let the opening remarks strike the key-note to the meeting. Anybody can speak or pray when a meeting has become lively, interesting, and warm. Blessed is the man who dares to take hold of the cold end of a prayer-meeting.

15. Would it not, in case no other method has been adopted, add to the interest and profit if the members, during the continuation of the year, would each select a dozen topics, with three or more proof texts from Scripture, such as are related to the needs, trials, and experiences of daily life, and then hand them to the pastor towards the end of the year? From these "themes from the pew," he would be able to pick out the right kind of topics for the needs of his people during the coming year and certainly the people themselves would be bound to take an interest in topics of their own choosing.

16. We may very briefly sum up the hints of Chapters 19, 21, 23, and 24 as follows: Let the people assemble some twenty minutes before the prayer-meeting for the practice of song and tarry some twenty minutes after it closes for social and religious greetings, etc. If this plan should be tried, it might be advisable, as in the case of the Brooklyn Tabernacle, to shorten the prayer-meeting to forty-five minutes. This, while making the whole session much less than two hours, would give such variety, interest, profit, and refreshment to each meeting as to make Wednesday evening the most delightful of all the inter-Sabbath days. And who does not spend more time than this at a social party without the least complaint?

Chapter 26

Daily Prayer-Meeting Topics

A very efficient aid to the improvement of the prayer-meeting will be the selection and use of just the right kind of subjects. The Presbytery of Peoria, at its last spring meeting, in order to assist those churches within its bounds desiring to use uniform topics, appointed a committee consisting of M. B. Lowrie, Elder John C. Grier, and the writer (Lewis Thompson) to prepare a list for the prayer-meetings of 1879. This list will be published at an early date so as to give all who may wish to use it an opportunity to do so. But it is not to be looked for that this list, or any other similarly prepared, shall secure for itself interdenominational circulation and use. And just here we meet one of the chief difficulties connected with the matter: there is no one authorized to prepare and publish such a list for the use of all the various denominations.

The difficulty in the way of uniform Sunday-School lessons was solved by the existence of an nondenominational Inter-State Association and that suggests that something similar might be done for the prayer-meeting. The "Y. M. C. A. of the United States and British Provinces" is nondenominational. They have an Executive Committee whose duty it is, among other things, to select the topics for their Daily Noon-day Prayer-Meetings and the annexed list, which is their selection, will show what admirable fitness they possess for just such a work as this. If those churches that favor uniformity were to adopt their Wednesday topics as the subjects for their evening prayer-meetings, the result aimed at would at once be secured and we should then have a list that all the denominations might be willing to use. If this should be done, it would be necessary for the committee to give their list a timely publication towards the close of each year.

Or, there is another way still by which to secure uniformity. The Evangelical Alliance is nondenominational and they have a standing committee who select the topics for the Week of Prayer. If they would prepare a list of subjects running through the year and publish it annually in October or November, then all the churches desiring to unite in its use might govern their actions accordingly. Either agency would do this work in an admirable and satisfactory manner.

The following is the list of the Y. M. C. A. for 1878 (Sunday topics are not included but Sunday-School lessons to study on Saturdays are):

Topics

January
1. Christ the Foundation. – 1 Cor. 3:9-16.
2. The Three Musts. – John 3:7, 14; Acts 4:12.
3. The First Commandment. – Ex. 20:3; Isa. 43:10-15.
4. The Stilling of the Tempest. – Mark 4:35-41.
5. Sunday-School Lesson: Rehoboam, First King of Judah; 2 Chr. 12:1-12, Golden Text: "*When he humbled himself, the wrath of the Lord turned from him*" (v.12).
6. Sunday.
7. Prayer: Prayer and Praise – Remembrance of personal and relative mercies; praise for the divine blessing on past privileges, and for a humble and contrite spirit. – Phil. 4:6-7; 1 Thess. 5:17-18.
8. Prayer: For the Church of Christ in all Lands – for its deliverance from error, for its increase in faith, holiness, and power as a witness for the Lord Jesus Christ, for the grace and guidance of the Holy Spirit. – Ps. 122.
9. Prayer: For Christian Families – for sick and afflicted members, for children at school, for all youth in our colleges and seminaries of learning, for young men entering upon the active business

of life, for those abroad, and for our sons and daughters openly confessing Christ. – Ps. 128.
10. Prayer: For Nations – for rulers, magistrates, and statesmen, for the army and navy, for all benevolent and philanthropic institutions, for religious liberty and the opening of doors wide and effectual for publishing the Gospel (1 Cor. 16:9), and for the reign of righteousness and peace. – Isa. 35:1-2; 1 Tim. 2:1-8.
11. Prayer: For Christian Missions to the Jews and Gentiles – for Sunday-schools and for the divine blessing on all Christian efforts to spread the glad tidings of the Gospel of Salvation. – Isa. 52:7-10; Matt. 28:18-20.
12. Prayer: For the circulation of the Bible, for the observance of the Sabbath, for the removal of intemperance, for the rescue of the fallen, and for the safety of those who travel by land and by water. – Ezek. 20:12-20; Luke 4:18-19; Acts 7:38.
13. Sunday-School Lesson: Asa, Faithful to his God. – 2 Chr. 14:1-11, Golden Text: *"Lord, it is nothing with Thee to help, whether with many, or with them that have no power"* (v. 11).
14. Sunday.
15. Working and Watching. – Neh. 4:1-21.
16. The Way of Life or of Death – Which? – Josh. 24:15; 1 Kings 18:21.
17. Is the Young Man Safe? – 2 Sam. 18:29-33.
18. The Sower. – Luke 8:5-8, 11-15.
19. God's Delight in Saving Sinners. – Ezek. 33:11; Eph. 2:4-8.
20. Sunday-School Lesson: The Covenant Renewed. – 2 Chr. 15:8-15, Golden Text: *"And they entered into a covenant to seek the LORD God of their fathers with all their heart and with all their soul"* (v. 12)
21. Sunday.
22. *"Our Father, which art in heaven (Matt. 6:9)."* – Acts 17:22-31; Gal. 4:4-7.
23. The Gain of the Hypocrite. – Job 27:8-10; Matt. 23:14.
24. *"Seekest thou great things for thyself? Seek them not."* (Jer. 45:5) Matt. 20:20-28; Mark 9:33-37.
25. Day of Prayer for Young Men in Colleges. – Prov. 3:1-7.
26. *"Come out of the man, thou unclean spirit."* (Mark 5:8) – Mark 5:1-20.
27. Sunday-School Lesson: Jehoshaphat's Prosperity. – 2 Chr. 17:1-10, Golden Text: *"And they taught in Judah, and had the book of the*

law of the Lord with them, and went about throughout all the cities of Judah, and taught the people." (v. 9).
28. Sunday.
29. The Inspiration of the Bible. – 2 Sam. 23:1-3; 2 Tim. 3:14-17; 2 Pet. 1:20-21.
30. Whither art thou going – to Nineveh or Tarshish? – Jonah 1.
31. Two Fearless Young Men. – Num. 14:2-10; 32:10-12.
32. The Tenderness of God. – Deut. 32:10-14.

February
1. Promise Meeting (2 Cor. 1:20): To the Sinner – John 6:37. To the Backslider – Jer. 3:22, To the Believer – Is. 41:10, 13; Rev. 21:4.
2. Sunday-School Lesson: Jehoshaphat Reproved. – 2 Chr. 19:1-9, Golden Text: *"There is no iniquity with the Lord our God, nor respect of persons, nor taking of gifts."* (v.7).
3. Sunday.
4. Self-Examination. – Ps. 77:6; 2 Cor. 1:12; 13:5.
5. *"What wilt thou say when He shall punish thee?"* (Jer. 13:21) – Prov. 11:21; Eccl. 8:11; Lam. 3:39; Nahum 1:2-8; Matt. 22:11-12; 2 Cor. 5:10-11.
6. The Lord Looketh on the Heart. – 1 Sam. 16:6-7.
7. The Second Commandment. – Ex. 20:4-6; Col. 3:1-5.
8. The Dead Brought to Life. – Mark 5:22-24, 35-43.
9. Sunday-School Lesson: Jehoshaphat Helped of God. – 2 Chr. 20:14-22, Golden Text: *"Believe in the Lord your God, so shall ye be established; believe His prophets, so shall ye prosper."* (v. 20).
10. Sunday.
11. *"What think ye of Christ?"* (Matt. 22:42) – Ps. 73:25; Isa. 53:2; Mark 8:29; John 3:2; 6:42; 20:28; 1 Pet. 2:7.
12. Opportunities Neglected. – Acts 24:24-27; 26:28.
13. A Promising Young Man and How He Failed. – 1 Sam. 9:2; 10:6-7; 28:16-19.
14. Salvation in Christ Alone. – Isa. 45:22; Acts 4:12.
15. The Unending Misery of the Lost and the Everlasting Joy of the Redeemed. – Is. 35:10; Mark 9:42-48.
16. Sunday-School Lesson: Joash Repairing the Temple. – 2 Chr. 24:4-13,

Golden Text: *"Joash was minded to repair the house of the Lord."* (v. 4).
17. Sunday.
18. *"Hallowed be Thy name."* (Matt. 6:9). – Ps. 113:1-3; Mal. 1:11.
19. Salvation is a Gift. – Rom. 6:23; 1 John 5:11.
20. Love Not the World. – Eccl. 2:1-11; 1 John 2:15-16.
21. Sins of Thought Offensive to God. – Gen. 6:5-7; 1 John 3:15.
22. Integrity in Civil Magistrates Insisted On. – Ex. 18:21; Neh. 5:15.
23. Sunday-School Lesson: Uzziah's Pride Punished. – 2 Chr. 26:16-23, Golden Text: *"Pride goeth before destruction, and a haughty spirit before a fall."* (Prov. 16:18).
24. Sunday.
25. The Bible in the Public Meeting. – Deut. 31:10-13; Neh. 8:1-8.
26. *"After this the judgment"* (Heb. 9:27). – Luke 12:5; Acts 17:31.
27. A Young Man Who Made the Right Choice. – Deut. 34:10-12; Heb. 11:24-27.
28. *"While they are yet speaking, I will hear."* (Is. 65:24). – Dan. 9:21-23; Luke 23:42-43; Acts 4:31; 12:5-10.

March

1. The Cleansing of the Leper. – Mark 1:40-45.
2. Sunday-School Lesson: Ahaz's Persistent Wickedness. – 2 Chr. 28:19-27, Golden Text: *"And in the time of his distress did he trespass yet more against the Lord: this is that King Ahaz."* (v. 22).
3. Sunday.
4. Sound Doctrine Enjoined. – John 7:17; 1 Tim. 4:16; 2 Tim. 4:1-4.
5. Christ the Way. – John 14:6; Heb. 10:19-23.
6. Ash Wednesday. *"Rend your heart and not your garments"* (Joel 2:13). – Joel 2:12-19; Ps. 51:17.
7. The Third Commandment. – Ex. 20:7; Matt. 5:33-37.
8. Christ's Tenderness to the Fallen. – Luke 7:36-50.
9. Sunday-School Lesson: Hezekiah's Good Reign. – 2 Chr. 29:1-11, Golden Text: *"And in every work that he began... he did it with all his heart and prospered."* (2 Chr. 31:21).
10. Sunday.
11. Brotherly Love. – 1 John 4:11-21.

12. I am Guilty and Need Pardon. – Rom. 3:23-26.
13. Blessedness of the Man Who Delights in the Word. – Ps. 1:1-3; James 1:25.
14. The Draw-Net. – Matt. 13:47-50.
15. The Healing of the Centurion's Servant. – Luke 7:1-10.
16. Sunday-School Lesson: Hezekiah and the Assyrians. – 2 Chr. 32:9-23, Golden Text: *"With him is an arm of flesh; but with us is the Lord our God, to help us, and to fight our battles."* (v. 8).
17. Sunday.
18. *"Thy kingdom come."* (Matt. 6:10). – Ps. 2; Rev. 11:15-17.
19. Christ the Truth. – John 17:3; 1 John 5:20.
20. The Good Fight. – 1 Tim. 6:12; 2 Tim. 4:7-8.
21. Confession Called Out. – Mark 5:25-34.
22. State of the Unsaved: Dead – Eph. 2:1, Lost – Luke 19:10, Condemned – John 3:19, Children of Wrath – Eph. 2:3, Without God – Eph. 2:12.
23. Sunday-School Lesson: Manasseh Brought to Repentance. – 2 Chr. 33:9-16, Golden Text: *"As many as I Love, I rebuke and chasten: be zealous, therefore, and repent."* (Rev. 3:19).
24. Sunday.
25. Christ our Substitute. – John 1:29; 2 Cor. 5:21; Gal. 2:20; Heb. 9:28.
26. National Disobedience. – 1 Sam. 12:15; Jer. 12:17.
27. Tampering with Sin. – Judg. 16:4-20.
28. Duties of Employers. – Eph. 6:9; Col. 4:1.
29. The Man with the Unclean Spirit. – Mark 1:23-27.
30. Sunday-School Lesson: Review of the Lessons for the Quarter.
31. Sunday.

April

1. Forbearing Grace. – Luke 13:6-9.
2. Christ the Life. – John 6:33-40.
3. *"None Righteous"* (Rom. 3:10) – Eccl. 7:20; Rom. 3:10-18.
4. The Fourth Commandment. – Ex. 20:8-11; Jer. 17:19-27.
5. Is God Ready to Pardon Me Now? – Ps. 86:5; Is. 1:18-20; 2 Cor. 6:2.
6. Sunday-School Lesson: Josiah's Early Piety. – 2 Chr. 34:1-7, Golden Text: *"Remember now thy Creator in the days of thy youth, while*

DAILY PRAYER-MEETING TOPICS

the evil days come not, nor the years draw nigh, when thou shalt say, I have no pleasure in them" (Eccl. 12:1).
7. Sunday.
8. Power of the Prayer of Faith. – Josh. 10:12-14; James 5:16-18; 1 John 5:14-15.
9. The New Heart. – Ezek. 36:26; Acts 15:9.
10. A Young Man Who Found Favor with God and Man. – Gen. 41:12-13, 38-45.
11. Duties of the Employed. – Col. 3:22-25; Titus 2:9-10.
12. *"Wilt thou be made whole?"* (John 5:6) – John 5:1-16.
13. Sunday-School Lesson: The Scriptures Found and Searched. – 2 Chr. 34:14-22, Golden Text: *"Search the Scriptures; for in them ye think ye have eternal life: and they are they which testify of Me."* (John 5:39).
14. Sunday
15. *"Thy will be done"* (Matt. 6:10). – Matt. 7:21; Rom. 2:13.
16. What to Lay Off and What to Put On. – Col. 3:8-15.
17. How Can a Man be Born Again? By Believing – 1 John 5:1, By Receiving – John 1:12-13, By the Spirit – Tit. 3:5, By the Word of God – Jam. 1:18.
18. *"Cast the net on the right side"* (John 21:6). – John 21:1-14.
19. Sufferings of Christ. – Isa. 52:13-15; 53:1-12.
20. Sunday-School Lesson: Jeremiah in Prison. – Jer. 33:1-9, Golden Text: *"Call unto Me, and I will answer thee, and show thee great and mighty things, which thou knowest not."* (v. 3).
21. Sunday.
22. Jesus' Resurrection. – Matt. 28:1-20.
23. The Sinner's Wealth. – Rom. 2:5-9.
24. One Who Trusted in Something Better than his Own Good Works. – Phil. 3:4-15.
25. The Unmerciful Servant. – Matt. 18:21-35.
26. *"Lord, save me."* (Matt. 14:30). – Matt. 14:22-33.
27. Sunday-School Lesson: The Rechabites. – Jer. 35.12-19, Golden Text: *"Will ye not receive instruction to hearken to my words? saith the Lord."* (v. 13).
28. Sunday.

29. *"God is our refuge"* (Ps. 46:1). – Ps. 46.
30. The Wicked Husbandmen. – Mark 12:1-12.

May

1. A Personal Savior. – Phil. 3:10; 2 Tim. 1:12.
2. The Believer's Home. – Ps. 17:15; Rev. 3:12; 21:25.
3. The Compassion of Jesus. – Matt. 9:35-38.
4. Sunday-School Lesson: The Captivity of Judah. – Jer. 52:1-11, Golden Text: *"Jerusalem hath grievously sinned; therefore she is removed"* (Lam. 1:8).
5. Sunday.
6. "Now." – Luke 14:17; Rom. 8:1; 2 Cor. 6:2; 1 John 3:2.
7. I am a Rebel, and Need to be Restored to the Divine Favor. – Isa. 53:6; Rom. 3:10-12.
8. A Young Man Who Despised the Promises of God. – Gen. 25:27-34; Heb. 12:16-17.
9. Laborers in the Vineyard. – Matt. 20:1-16.
10. The Woman Loosed from Her Infirmity. – Ps. 145:14; Luke 13:10-17.
11. Sunday-School Lesson: The Captives in Babylon. – Dan. 1:8-17, Golden Text: *"A good understanding have all they that do His commandments"* (Ps. 111:10).
12. Sunday.
13. The Testimony of the Man Born Blind. – John 9.
14. Choose. – Deut. 30:15-19.
15. We Must Forsake our Sins. – Is. 55:7; Ezek. 18:30-32.
16. The Ten Virgins. – Matt. 25:1-13.
17. Able to Keep. – Ps. 121; Jude 24.
18. Sunday-School Lesson: Nebuchadnezzar's Dream. – Dan. 2:36-45, Golden Text: *"There is a God in heaven that revealeth secrets"* (v. 28).
19. Sunday.
20. Searching the Scriptures. – John 5:38-40; Acts 17:11-12.
21. God as a Suppliant. – Is. 65:2; Hos. 11:1-9.
22. Christ an Example of Humility. – John 13:1-15.
23. Unbelief. – Ps. 78:17-22; 1 John 5:10-11.
24. The Withered Hand Restored. – Luke 6:6-11.
25. Sunday-School Lesson: The Fiery Furnace. – Dan. 3:21-27, Golden

Text: *"Our God whom we serve is able to deliver us from the burning fiery furnace"* (v. 17).
26. Sunday.
27. Christ Coming for His Saints. – John 14:1-3; 1 Cor. 15:51-54; 1 Thess. 4:13-18.
28. *"But they made light of it"* (Matt. 22:5). – Luke 14:15-24.
29. The Prizes of Christian Warfare. – Rev. 3:5, 12, 21.
30. Ascension Day. – Luke 24:44-53.
31. Encouraging Promises. – Matt. 9:29; 10:22; Rom. 10:9; Jam. 1:12.

June.

1. Sunday-School Lesson: The Handwriting on the Wall. – Dan. 5:22-31, Golden Text: *"Thou art weighed in the balances, and art found wanting."* (v. 27).
2. Sunday
3. Self-Denial. – Gen. 12:1-5; Heb. 11:8-10.
4. How Shall the Sinner Escape? – Heb. 2:3; 1 Pet. 4:18.
5. Evil Thoughts – How can I be delivered from them? – Matt. 15:19-20; 2 Cor. 10:5.
6. The Fifth Commandment. – Ex. 20:12; Luke 2:51.
7. Self-Purification Impossible. – Prov. 20:9; Jer. 2:22; 13:23.
8. Sunday-School Lesson: Daniel in the Lions' Den. – Dan. 6:14-23, Golden Text: *"My God hath sent His angel, and hath shut the lions' mouths, that they have not hurt me"* (v. 22).
9. Sunday.
10. What Christ Does for the Believer: He Died for Me – John 10:11, He Seeks Me – Ezek. 34:11, He Gives Me Rest – Ps. 23:2a, He Knows Me – John 10:27, He Leads Me – Ps. 23:2b, He Carries Me – Is. 40:11, He Feeds Me – John 21:15, He Heals Me – Ezek. 34:16, He Makes Me a Blessing – Ezek. 34:26, He Comes for Me – John 14:3.
11. Seek ye the Lord. – Amos 5:4-8.
12. The Temple of God. – 1 Cor. 3:16-17; 2 Cor. 6:16.
13. *"Where are the nine?"* (Luke 17:17) – Luke 17:11-19.
14. The Sinner Invited. – Matt. 11:28-30; John 6:37.
15. Sunday-School Lesson: Messiah's Kingdom. – Dan. 7:9-14, Golden

Text: "*Thy throne, O God, is for ever and ever; the scepter of thy kingdom is a right scepter.*" (Ps. 45:6).

16. Sunday.
17. The Word a Light. – Ps. 119:105, 130; Prov. 6:23.
18. A Promise Given and a Choice Required. – Jer. 29:13; Matt. 6:24.
19. On What Are You Building? – Matt. 7:24-29.
20. Fruitfulness. – John 15:1-5.
21. "*If thou canst believe*" (Mark 9:23). – Mark 9:14-29.
22. Sunday-School Lesson: The Decree of Cyrus. – 2 Chr. 36:22-23, Golden Text: "*Speak ye comfortably to Jerusalem, and cry unto her, that her warfare is accomplished, that her iniquity is pardoned*" (Is. 40:2).
23. Sunday.
24. "*Give us this day our daily bread.*" (Matt. 6:11). – Ps. 34:10; Prov. 30:8-9.
25. An Important Question Answered. – Ps. 15.
26. My Besetting Sin – How Can I Get Strength to Overcome It? – 1 Cor. 9:27; Heb. 12:1-4.
27. The Christian in the World. – Matt. 5:13-16.
28. Decision Necessary to the Service of God. – Luke 9:62; 2 Chr. 15:12.
29. Sunday-School Lesson: Review of the Lessons for the Quarter.
30. Sunday.

July

1. The Work of the Spirit. – Rom. 8:14-17; 1 Cor. 2:9-16.
2. Where is your Brother? – Gen. 4:9; Ezek. 33:8-9.
3. What Christ Says to Every Unconverted Young Man. – Luke 7:11-16.
4. God's Children Free. – John 8:31-36.
5. The Raising of Lazarus. – John 11:1-45.
6. Sunday-School Lesson: Birth of Christ the Lord. – Luke 2:8-20, Golden Text: "*For unto you is born this day, in the city of David, a Saviour, which is Christ the Lord.*" (v. 11).
7. Sunday.
8. Christ Coming with His Saints. – Col. 3:4; 2 Thess. 1:7-10; Jude 14-15.
9. "*Wait on the Lord*" (Ps. 27:14). – Is. 40:28-31; Lam. 3:25-26.
10. Invitations Refused. – Prov. 1:24-28; Luke 14:15-24.
11. "*Give ye them to eat.*" (Mark 6:37). – Luke 9:12-17; John 21:15-17.

12. Christ's Willingness to Receive Sinners. – Luke 9:11; 15:2; John 6:37.
13. Sunday-School Lesson: The Childhood of Jesus. – Luke 2:40-52, Golden Text: *"And Jesus increased in wisdom and stature, and in favor with God and man."* (v. 52).
14. Sunday.
15. Christ Is Able To: Perform All He Promises – Rom. 4:21, Save to the Uttermost – Heb. 7:25, Make Us Stand – Rom. 14:4, Keep Us from Falling – Jude 24, Keep What is Committed to Him – 2 Tim. 1:12, Succor [help] the Tempted – Heb. 2:18, Make All Grace Abound – 2 Cor. 9:8, Do Exceeding Abundantly Above All that We Ask or Think – Eph. 3:20.
16. *"All that believe are justified"* (Acts 13:39). – Acts 13:38-39; Rom. 4:5; Gal. 2:16.
17. Seeking the Lost. – Luke 19:1-10.
18. The Sixth Commandment. – Ex. 20:13; Matt. 5:21-22.
19. *"Have mercy on me."* (Luke 18:38). – Mark 10:46-52.
20. Sunday-School Lesson: Ministry of John the Baptist. – Luke 3:15-22; Golden Text: *"For he shall be great in the sight of the Lord, and shall drink neither wine nor strong drink"* (Luke 1:15).
21. Sunday.
22. The Word Made Plain. – Ps. 119:18; Eph. 1:17-23.
23. Good News – Poor Men Made Rich. – Is. 55:1-3; Rev. 21:7.
24. In What Men should Glory. – Jer. 9:23-24; Gal. 6:14.
25. The Law of Growth in the Kingdom of God. – Mark 4:26-29; 2 Pet. 3:18.
26. Invitation to All. – 2 Cor. 5:20-21; 6:1-2; Rev. 22:17.
27. Sunday-School Lesson: Jesus at Nazareth. – Luke 4:16-30, Golden Text: *"And they were astonished at His doctrine; for His word was with power."* (v. 32).
28. Sunday.
29. The Lord our Helper. – Deut. 31:6-8; Ps. 20.
30. *"Learn of me"* – Matt. 11:29.
31. Evil Effects of Bad Company. – Gen. 13:12-13; 19:1, 12-28.

August

1. *"Humbleness of mind"* (Col. 3:12). – Col. 3:12-14.
2. The Healing of One Deaf and Dumb. – Mark 7:31-37.

THE PRAYER-MEETING AND ITS IMPROVEMENT

3. Sunday-School Lesson: The Draught of Fishes. – Luke 5:1-11, Golden Text: *"And when they had brought their ships to land, they forsook all, and followed Him."* (v. 11).
4. Sunday.
5. The Weapon of Our Warfare. – Jer. 23:29; Eph. 6:17; Heb. 4:12.
6. The Rich Fool. – Luke 12:16-21.
7. An Ambitious Young Man and His Untimely End. – 2 Sam. 15:1-5, 13-14; 18:6-15.
8. The Seventh Commandment. – Ex. 20:14; Eph. 5:3-7.
9. Victory over the Devil. – Gen. 3:15; Matt. 4:1-11; 1 John 2:14.
10. Sunday-School Lesson: The Centurion's Faith. – Luke 7:1-10, Golden Text: *"According to your faith be it unto you."* (Matt. 9:29).
11. Sunday.
12. Despising the Word. – Prov. 13:13; Heb. 2:1-3.
13. Two Companies and Two Ends. – Ex. 23:2; Matt. 7:13-14; Luke 16:22-23; Heb. 12:22-24.
14. What it is to know Christ. – John 17:3; Phil. 3:7-11.
15. Hearing God's Call. – 1 Sam. 3:1-10.
16. "He will abundantly pardon." (Is. 55:7). – Neh. 9:16-17.
17. Sunday-School Lesson: The Widow of Nain. – Luke 7:11-17, Golden Text: "And when the Lord saw her, He had compassion on her, and said unto her, Weep not." (v.13).
18. Sunday.
19. Christ Coming in Judgment. – Matt. 25:31-46.
20. *"Escape for thy life"* (Gen. 19:17). – Gen. 19:15-17.
21. Young Men – Their Rule for Right Living. – Josh. 1:8; Ps. 119:9.
22. Duties of Parents to Children. – Deut. 6:6-9; Eph. 6:4.
23. The Great Change. – Zech. 3:1-7.
24. Sunday-School Lesson: The Friend of Sinners. – Luke 7:40-50, Golden Text: *"This man receiveth sinners"* (Luke 15:2).
25. Sunday.
26. Seven Results of Abiding in Christ: Fruit, Answered Prayer, Love, Obedience, Joy, Fellowship, Service. – John 15:5-16.
27. The Lost Piece of Money. – Luke 15:1-2; 8-10.
28. Individual Responsibility. – Rom. 14:10-12; 2 Cor. 5:10.
29. The Waiting Lord. – Song of Sol. 5:2; Rev. 3:20.

30. Christ Lives in the Believer. – Gal. 2:20; Eph. 3:14-21.
31. Sunday-School Lesson: Return of the Seventy. – Luke 10:17-24, Golden Text: *"Blessed are the eyes which see the things that ye see"* (v. 23).

September

1. Sunday.
2. *"He opened to us the Scriptures"* (Luke 24:32). – Luke 24:13-32.
3. The Way Out of the Ditch. – Jer. 3:12-13; Hos. 14:1-4.
4. *"Your sin will find you out."* (Num. 32:23). – Gen. 44:16-34
5. The Eighth Commandment. – Ex. 20:15; Lev. 19:11-13.
6. Christ's Help in Temptation. – 2 Cor. 12:9; Heb. 2:18.
7. Sunday-School Lesson: The Good Samaritan. – Luke 10:30-37, Golden Text: *"Thou shalt love thy neighbor as thyself."* (Gal. 5:14).
8. Sunday.
9. *"Forgive us our debts as we forgive our debtors."* (Matt. 6:12). Matt. 18:21-22; Mark 11:25.
10. Idleness. – Prov. 24:30-34.
11. An Exhortation to a Young Man. – 1 Tim. 4:12-16
12. Love the Impulse to Labor. – John 21:15-17; 2 Cor. 5:14-15.
13. Invitation to the Thirsty. – Isa. 55:1-9.
14. Sunday-School Lesson: Importunity in Prayer. – Luke 11:5-13, Golden Text: *"Men ought always to pray, and not to faint"* (Luke 18:1).
15. Sunday.
16. God – the Deliverer of His People. – Ex. 14:10-31.
17. The Sinner's Condemnation. – John 3:17-21.
18. A Zeal for Christ which Consumes Self. – Luke 9:23; 2 Cor. 5:14-15; 1 Thess. 2:8.
19. The Aged – Prayer and Promise. – Ps. 71:1-19; Prov. 16:31; Is. 46:4.
20. *"Do all to the glory of God."* (1 Cor. 10:31). – 1 Cor. 10:31-33; Rom. 15:3.
21. Sunday-School Lesson: Warning against Covetousness. – Luke 12:13-23, Golden Text: *"Take heed, and beware of covetousness"* (v. 15).
22. Sunday.
23. Indwelling and Comfort of the Holy Spirit. – John 16:7-14; 20:22; Acts 2:4.

24. Christ's Mission. – 1 Tim. 1:15.
25. True to God, Regardless of Consequences. – Dan. 3:13-30.
26. Neglect of the Poor is a Neglect of Christ. – Matt. 25:42-45; Mark 9:41.
27. Nothing too Hard for God. – Ps. 130:1-5; Jer. 32:17, 27.
28. Sunday-School Lesson: Review of the Lessons for the Quarter.
29. Sunday.
30. God's Word in Us. – Ps. 119:11; Jer. 20:9; Col. 3:16.

October

1. Too Late. – Luke 19:41-44; Heb. 3:17-19.
2. Wisdom. – Prov. 2:1-9; James 1:5.
3. The Ninth Commandment. – Ex. 20:16; Ps. 15:1-4.
4. Sowing and Reaping. – Gal. 6:7-8.
5. Sunday-School Lesson: Warning against Formalism. – Luke 13:22-30, Golden Text: "*Strive to enter in at the strait gate: for many, I say unto you, will seek to enter in, and shall not be able,*" (v. 24).
6. Sunday.
7. Tokens of Our Love to God. – John 14:21-23; 1 John 2:15.
8. Jabez's Prayer. – 1 Chr. 4:9-10.
9. A Young Man Who Sought only this World's Joys. – Luke 15:11-24.
10. The Question Every Man Must Answer. – Matt. 27:22.
11. The Savior We Need Was Offered Up. – Rom. 3:10-26.
12. Sunday-School Lesson: The Gospel Feast. – Luke 14:15-24, Golden Text: "*Blessed is he that shall eat bread in the kingdom of God.*" (v. 15).
13. Sunday.
14. Things We Know. – Rom. 7:18; 8:28; 2 Tim. 1:12; 1 John 5:13.
15. Safe Voyage – If Christ is on Board. – Mark 4:35-41.
16. Whole-hearted for Christ. – Luke 9:57-62.
17. "*At Thy word I will let down the net.*" (Luke 5:5). – Luke 5:1-11.
18. Exhortation to Watchfulness. – 1 Thess. 5:6-8.
19. Sunday-School Lesson: The Prodigal Son. – Luke 15:11-24, Golden Text: "*I am poor and needy; yet the Lord thinketh upon me*" (Ps. 40:17).
20. Sunday.

21. *"Lead us not into temptation, but deliver us from evil"* (Matt. 6:13). – 1 Cor. 10:13; 2 Tim. 4:18; Jas. 1:13-15; 2 Pet. 2: 9.
22. The Two Future States. – Luke 16:19-31.
23. How a Young Man made his Life Successful. – Acts 7:57-59; 26:9-23; 2 Cor. 5:13-14.
24. The Pharisee and the Publican. – Luke 18:9-14.
25. *"The Lamb of God"* (John 1:36). – John 1:29; Rev. 5:12-13; 6:15-17.
26. Sunday-School Lesson: The Rich Man and Lazarus. – Luke 16:19-31, Golden Text: *"The wicked is driven away in his wickedness; but the righteous hath hope in his death."* (Prov. 14:32).
27. Sunday.
28. Teaching and Keeping God's Word. – Deut. 11:18-25.
29. The Call to the Backslider. – Jer. 2:5, 13, 19; 3:12-14.
30. Ruined by Evil Company. – 2 Chr. 10:1-15; 12:13-16.
31. Profession without Fruit is an Offence. – Mark 11:12-14; John 15:2.

November

1. The Wanderer's Cry. – Ps. 51.
2. Sunday-School Lesson: The Ten Lepers. – Luke 17:11-19, Golden Text: *"And Jesus answering said, Were there not ten cleansed? but where are the nine?"* (v.17).
3. Sunday.
4. Promise Meeting. – Matt. 28:20; John 14:3; Acts 1:8; 2 Pet. 1:4.
5. Who are Haters of God? – John 15:17-25; Rom. 8:7-8.
6. A Young Man's Wise Choice. – 1 Kings 3:5-15.
7. The Tenth Commandment. – Ex. 20:17; Heb. 13:5.
8. *"We will hear thee again"* (Acts 17:32). – Prov. 27:1.
9. Sunday-School Lesson: Whom the Lord Receives. – Luke 18:9-17, Golden Text: *"Verily I say unto you, Whosoever shall not receive the kingdom of God as a little child, shall in no wise enter therein."* (v. 17).
10. Sunday.
11. Young Men – their Power for Evil. – 1 Kings 11:28; 12:26-30; 13:33 -34; Acts 7:57-60; 8:1-3.
12. Young Men – Their Power for Good. – Prov. 20:29; Eph. 6:10-11; 1 John 2:13-14.
13. Something Stronger than the Strength of Young Men. – Is. 40:28-31.

14. How to Reach Young Men. – John 1:35-51.
15. Young Men – Their Special Temptations. – Eccl. 11:9-10; 2 Tim. 2:22.
16. The Pattern for Young Men. – Luke 2:42-52; Acts 10:38-43.
17. Sunday-School Lesson: Zacchaeus the Publican. – Luke 19:1-10, Golden Text: *"The Son of Man is come to seek and to save that which was lost."* (v. 10).
18. Sunday.
19. Baptism of the Spirit for Service. – Acts 1:8; 2:4; 4:31.
20. When Do Men Cry Unto the Lord? – Ps. 107:5-6, 12-13, 18-19, 27-28.
21. A Life Well Begun. – 2 Chr. 34:1-8, 29-33.
22. The Lesson of Patience. – Jas. 5:7-11.
23. Invitation and Warning. – Prov. 1:24-33; Is. 1:18.
24. Sunday-School Lesson: Judaism Overthrown. – Luke 21:8-21, Golden Text: *"And when He was come near, He beheld the city, and wept over it."* (Luke 19:41).
25. Sunday.
26. Profit in Using the Word. – Is. 55:10-11; 2 Tim. 3:12-17.
27. Repentance. – Ezek. 18:32; Matt. 9:13; Acts 5:31.
28. A Young Man in Whom the World Found no Fault except by His Faith. – Dan. 6:1-5, 25-28; Phil. 2:15.
29. *"The Sacrifice of Praise"* (Heb. 13:15). – Ps. 148; Heb. 13:15-16; Rev. 7:12.
30. Halting Between Two Opinions. – Joshua 24:15; 1 Kings 18:21.
31. Sunday-School Lesson: The Lord's Supper. – Luke 22:10-20, Golden Text: *"For as often as ye eat this bread, and drink this cup, ye do show the Lord's death till He come."* (1 Cor. 11:26).

December

1. Sunday.
2. The Imagination: Corrupt – Rom. 1:21; Deut. 29:19-20, Redeemed – Isa. 26:3 ("Mind," in this passage means "imagination" or "thought"); Phil. 4:7.
3. God our Searcher. – 1 Chr. 28:9; Ps. 139:23-24.
4. Some Things Money Cannot Buy: Redemption – 1 Pet. 1:18-19, The Gift of the Spirit Acts 8:18-24, The Heavenly Inheritance – 1 Pet. 1:3-5.

5. The Pounds. – Luke 19:11-27.
6. I am a Slave to Sin and Need to be Set Free. – Phil. 2:7-9; Heb. 2:14, 15.
7. Sunday-School Lesson: The Cross. – Luke 23:33-46, Golden Text: *"God forbid that I should glory, save in the cross of our Lord Jesus Christ"* (Gal. 6:14).
8. Sunday.
9. Justification. – Is. 53:11; Rom. 5:8-10; 8:33.
10. Grieve Not the Holy Spirit. – Gen. 6:3; Is. 63:10; 1 Thess. 5:19.
11. A Young Man's Foolish Choice. – Mark 10:17-22.
12. Idle Words. – Matt. 12:36; Eph. 4:29-31.
13. Joy over Deliverance. – Acts 8:5-8.
14. Sunday-School Lesson: The Walk to Emmaus. – Luke 24:13-32, Golden Text: *"And they said one to another, Did not our heart burn within us, while He talked with us by the way, and while He opened to us the Scriptures?"* (v. 32).
15. Sunday.
16. The Word is *"written, that ye might believe"* (John 20:31). – 2 Tim. 3:15; 1 John 5:13.
17. A Sinner Awakened and Saved. – Acts 16:22-34.
18. Christ as a Pattern for Young Men. – Phil. 2:5-16.
19. Riches Do Not Satisfy. – Ps. 49:6-7, 11-13; Eccl. 5:10-11; 1 Tim. 6:17-19.
20. Help Comes from God. – Ps. 89:19; 142:4-5.
21. Sunday-School Lesson: The Savior's Last Words. – Luke 24:44-53, Golden Text: *"Lo, I am with you alway, even unto the end of the world. Amen."* (Matt. 28:20).
22. Sunday.
23. Christ – the Fulfillment of Scripture. – Matt. 5:17; Luke 24:27; Rev. 19:10.
24. Redemption. – Gal. 4:4-5; 1 Pet. 1:18-19.
25. Glad Tidings. – Luke 2:1-20.
26. *"Think on these Things."* (Phil. 4:8). – Phil. 4:8-9; Heb. 2:1.
27. *"Mighty to Save."* – Isa. 63:1.
28. Sunday-School Lesson: Review of the Lessons for the Quarter.
29. Sunday.
30. *"For Thine is the kingdom, the power and the glory"* (Matt. 6:13). – 1 Chr. 29:10-13; Ps. 62:11; Rev. 5:13.

31. How Shall We Number Our Days and Years? – Ps. 90:12; Eccl. 9:10; Eph. 5:15-17.

"Did not our heart burn within us, while He talked with us by the way, and while He opened to us the Scriptures?"
(Luke 24:32)

"Now unto Him that is able to keep you from falling, and to present you faultless before the presence of His glory with exceeding joy, to the only wise God our Saviour, be glory and majesty, dominion and power, both now and ever. Amen."
(Jude 24-25)

Bibliography

Chamberlain, H. B. (1877). *Handbook of Bible Readings*. F. H. Revell.

Finney, C. G. (1908). *Autobiography of Charles G. Finney: A Lifetime of Evangelical Preaching to Christians across America, Revealed.*

Hill, J. C. (1877). *Hints on Bible Readings*. Not Known.

Hitchcock, R. D. (1871). *Hitchcock's Complete Analysis of the Holy Bible*. New York: A. J. Johnson.

Inglis, J. (1860). *The Bible Text Cyclopedia*. Not known.

Locke, J., & Dodd, W. (2016). *A Common-place Book to the Holy Bible or the Scripture's Sufficiency Practically Demonstrated. Wherein the Substance of Scripture Respecting Doctrine, Worship and Manners Is Reduced to Its Proper Heads.* Wentworth Press.

Macmillan, H. (1871). *Bible Teachings in Nature*. London: Macmillan and Co.

Mattison, H. (1866). *The Resurrection of the Body*. Perkinpine & Higgins.

Thompson, L. O. (n.d.). *How to Conduct Prayer-Meetings, or an Account of some meetings that have been Held.*

Trevelyan, G. O. (1876). *The Life and Letters of Lord Macauley*. London: Longmans Green and Co.

White, J. (1878). *Eighteen Christian Centuries; Second Edinburgh Edition*. New York: D. Appleton and Company.

Other Similar Titles

The Necessity of Prayer, by E. M. Bounds

Persistent prayer is a mighty movement of the soul toward God, and it stirs the deepest forces of the soul toward the throne of heavenly grace. It is the ability to hold on, press on, and wait. Restless desire, restful patience, and strength of grasp are all embraced in it. Prayer is not an incident or a performance but a passion of soul. It is not a want or half-needed desire but a sheer necessity.

Available where books are sold.

The Essentials of Prayer, by E. M. Bounds

Christians who pray well, who bring the largest things to pass, and who move God to do great things, are those who are entirely given over to God in their praying. God wants, and must have, all that there is in us. We must be wholehearted people through whom he can work out his purposes and plans concerning us. God must have us in our entirety. No double-minded people need apply. No vacillating person can be used. No person with a divided allegiance to God, the world, and self can do the praying that is needed. Holiness is wholeness, and so God wants holy people – wholehearted and true – for his service and for the work of praying.

This book challenges the reader to first make sure he is ready to pray, and it also shows from Scripture when and how we ought to pray. E. M. Bounds examines the lack of prayer and its causes, but he also includes examples of answered prayer to give hope to those who feel like their prayers aren't being answered. Some may experience guilt for their lack and inconsistency of prayer, but sincere Christians will also be stirred in their heart to pray, and to pray well.

Available where books are sold.

Prevailing Prayer, by Dwight L. Moody

This book is a comprehensive study on the subject of prayer, and will show you that there are nine elements which are essential to true prayer. These elements are as follows:

Adoration, Confession, Restitution, Thanksgiving, Forgiveness, Unity, Faith, Petition, Submission

Dwight Moody expounds on these nine elements in this volume, using illustrations and stories to validate what he is saying and to help make the truths in this book stick.

Available where books are sold.

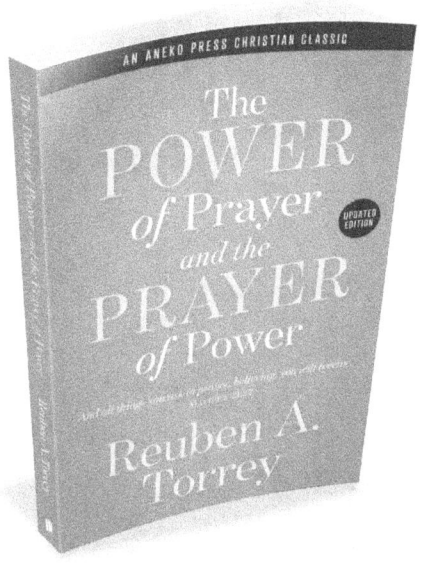

The Power of Prayer and the Prayer of Power,
by Reuben A. Torrey

Prayer is the key that unlocks all the storehouses of God's infinite grace and power. All that God is, and all that God has, is at the disposal of prayer; but we must use the key. Prayer can do anything that God can do, and since God can do anything, prayer is omnipotent. No one can stand against the person who knows how to pray, who meets all the conditions of prevailing prayer, and who really prays, and if they are willing to pay the price. The price is prayer, much prayer, much real prayer, prayer in the Holy Spirit.

Available where books are sold.

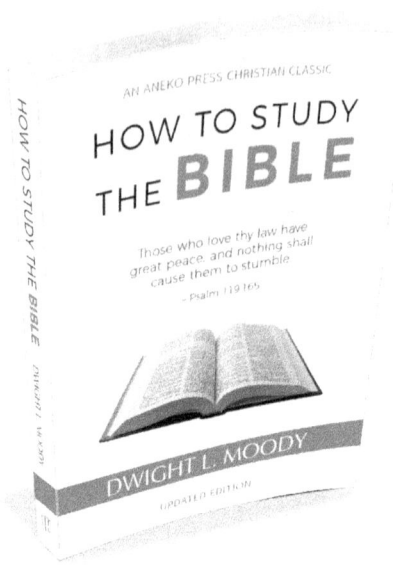

How to Study the Bible, by Dwight L. Moody

There is no situation in life for which you cannot find some word of consolation in Scripture. If you are in affliction, if you are in adversity and trial, there is a promise for you. In joy and sorrow, in health and in sickness, in poverty and in riches, in every condition of life, God has a promise stored up in His Word for you.

This classic book by Dwight L. Moody brings to light the necessity of studying the Scriptures, presents methods which help stimulate excitement for the Scriptures, and offers tools to help you comprehend the difficult passages in the Scriptures. To live a victorious Christian life, you must read and understand what God is saying to you. Moody is a master of using stories to illustrate what he is saying, and you will be both inspired and convicted to pursue truth from the pages of God's Word.

Available where books are sold.

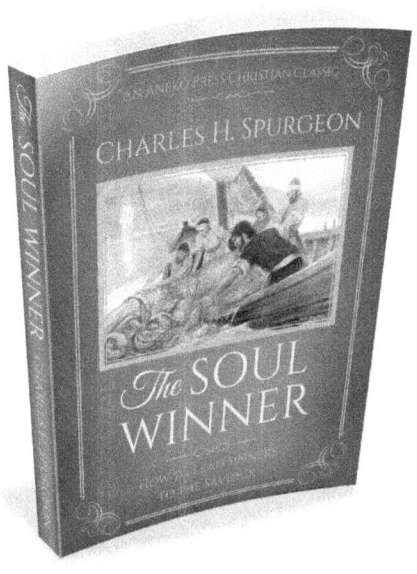

The Soul Winner, by Charles H. Spurgeon

As an individual, you may ask, How can I, an average person, do anything to reach the lost? Or if a pastor, you may be discouraged and feel ineffective with your congregation, much less the world. Or perhaps you don't yet have a heart for the lost. Whatever your excuse, it's time to change. Overcome yourself and learn to make a difference in your church and the world around you. It's time to become an effective soul winner for Christ.

As Christians, our main business is to win souls. But, in Spurgeon's own words, "like shoeing-smiths, we need to know a great many things. Just as the smith must know about horses and how to make shoes for them, so we must know about souls and how to win them for Christ." Learn about souls, and how to win them, from one of the most acclaimed soul winners of all time.

Available where books are sold.

www.ingramcontent.com/pod-product-compliance
Lightning Source LLC
Chambersburg PA
CBHW070139080526
44586CB00015B/1758